YOUR LIFE
IN THEATRE

A self-help guide for all stages of your career

by
Chris Grady

Produced with support from Arts Council England
Grant for the Arts Programme 2013

Orders: Please contact Chris Grady at ChrisGrady.org or via the email
address chrisgradyorg@gmail.com.

The cover image is by Zoe Barnes from a production by Creative Cow.
Take a Bow after a production of The Rivals by Richard Brinsley Sheridan
www.creativecow.co.uk
http://1x.com/member/zoelouisebarnes/photos/all
My thanks for permission to use this image to celebrate theatre and the
audience.

ISBN: 9781910202487

First published in 2014 by ChrisGrady.org
Copyright © 2014 Chris Grady. All rights reserved.

Typeset for Chris Grady by the BookPublishingAcademy.co.uk

Printed in Great Britain for How2become Ltd by:
CMP (uk) Limited, Poole, Dorset.

CONTENTS

"A no-nonsense guide to the pitfalls of a difficult profession from a man who knows the business inside out: chatty, informative and intensely personal."

Gregory Doran
Artistic Director, Royal Shakespeare Company

Chris Grady is available for one-to-one coaching and freelance consulting.

For more information please contact Chris at:
www.ChrisGrady.org
chris@chrisgrady.org

Introduction

This short book is the result of nearly 40 years working in the arts, and the most recent 7 years offering a formal series of monthly one-on-one CGO Surgeries for creative artists. The Surgeries are a mix of mentoring, coaching, consulting and listening. In the CGO Surgeries I aim to use some of the skills that I have learned over the years to listen, support, at times cajole, and maybe inspire each person. Sometimes it works really well – and they go off with a spring in their step, or an action plan. Sometimes it works quite well – and they take a couple of helpful hints or realisations, and maybe I don't hear from them again. And very occasionally nothing useful happens.

This book gathers some of the ideas we cover in our conversations. I initially titled this book "Coffee or Chamomile Tea", seeking to suggest that the informal conversations are either stimulating or soothing – whichever is needed at the time. My publisher, the amazing Richard McMunn of the Book Publishing Academy www.bookpublishingacademy.co.uk, rightly suggested that might not hit high in google searching – so welcome to *Your Life in Theatre*.

Those who attend a CGO Surgery fit, very generally, into three types:

Aspiring/Emerging – maybe in need of some very concrete pointers, contacts, next steps.

Inspired/Overwhelmed – maybe in need of clarity, next step, time-life-work balance.

Despairing/Stuck – maybe in need of a new direction or re-inspiring.

This sometimes flows with age – the young "tigger"/ enthusiast; the career-seeker feeling overwhelmed; and the experienced/wise/tired professional. But we can all feel old at whatever age, and hopefully we can all feel aspirational – although it may take a bit more coffee.

Within the sections of this book, I have used William Shakespeare's "Seven Ages of Man" speech from *As You Like It*. Partly to inspire me, and partly because I love the fact that we (or our ideas) enter this world mewling and puking....

"Aspiring and Emerging" covers around 50% of the book – because we all benefit from a reminder of some of the basics. I am light on the "Overwhelmed and Despairing", because that moves further away from general thoughts and more towards Personal Coaching. I am delighted to talk one-on-one with people as part of my CGO Surgery or Coaching practice.

This book is made possible through a small Grant for the Arts award to support the CGO Surgeries and extend their reach. Initial sessions in London have now spread to days in several other English and Scottish cities. This draft edition of the book gives access to what's bubbling around my head, whether or not people have access to a Surgery.

I have sought to make most stories and references anonymous. The Surgeries themselves are very specific, personal, and confidential. This book is therefore more general and the reader needs to find what's relevant to their own situation. Or come to a Surgery!

Thanks for opening this...

Chris Grady
June 2014

How to Use This Book

This book is drawn from five sources:

- Blogs written for Whatsonstage in the last 2-3 years.
- Articles written by me over the last few years.
- Ideas that have flown with the Coffee.
- Reading I have done to help at the Chamomile Tea / soothing moments.
- Wisdom from others, which I hope I have credited.

This is a "dip in" book, and the index and contents pages may be the first place to start.

On some pages there is space for your own writing/notes – because as you read one paragraph a completely different inspiring thought may come to you. Let it flow. It may be the solution to a problem, a great new idea, or the final item for your shopping list – each needs to come out.

The Blogs are slightly edited down from their original brain-dump/publication. I have then tried to pick out salient ideas in the blog that have a more universal application.

I have spent a lot of time in the last 3 years writing about Edinburgh Festival Fringe and Musical Theatre – because that's been an ongoing part of my life. So you may wish to "universalise" some of the specifics.

I have changed the odd name if I feel now, on reflection, that it should be more anonymous. The dates of writing are given as YYMMDD. My own way of filing stuff so it ends up in date order. Where something has changed significantly I have added a comment.

How to Make the Book Better

Give me feedback.

Give me any old wives' tales or fantastic tips you have received from past wise ones. Allow me to weave them into the next edition of this book.

Let me know if any of the articles, thoughts, suggestions ring true – and maybe give me other examples of successful practice from your own artform.

Use it, quote from it, and pass anything useful on. You have absolute permission. All I would ask is due credit, as I hope I have done myself.

Give me any corrections where I have made a real mistake. These can then be incorporated into the 1st complete edition – which will include some cartoons and illustrations I have been offered to complement the work.

Thank you.

Warning for Actors

This book does not give you acting lessons. It is not a technique study guide. It presumes you are a fine actor. This book is designed for creatives who would like to improve their chances by exploring the "business" of showbusiness. It is designed for artists and creative practitioners who are taking their own lives and careers in their own hands.

Acknowledgements

I am indebted to two people for putting up with me through thick and thin: Helen Grady, who was a wonderful person to share my early creative and personal journey with from Bristol, via Plymouth, then Edinburgh, Inverness and on to Buxton. She continues to be my most supportive critic, and has taken time to assess this book as an actress and a parent who brought up an actor and a singer (our children Michael and Anna) as they trod the path through school, conservatoire and into the big wide world. Thank you – no-one could ask for a better ex-wife. And to Kath Burlinson, to whom I am now married and with whom I share my present creative life. She has introduced me to so much in my middle years and it is a joy to share her journey with the Authentic Artist Collective www.authenticartist.co.uk and her amazing extended international family of performers. Thank you so much – you are inspiring.

Most of what you will find in this book came from the work I learned under two inspiring early leaders – Peter Tod, my boss at Bristol Hippodrome, and Gordon Stratford, my boss at the Theatre Royal, Plymouth. Both trusted me with far too much responsibility at an early age. They shared a passion for the art of theatre, a love of the theatre family, and respect for the audience. Thank you. And recently I have revisited so much of this youthful experience in my older years under the caring, creative leadership of Colin Blumenau at the Theatre Royal Bury St Edmunds – whose attention to detail was and is amazing. This attention to detail is matched by Sir Cameron Mackintosh who showed me time after time when

I worked for him that a producer, or anyone involved in the creation of successful theatre, must think of the art first. Take care of the art (and the pennies) and the pounds take care of themselves.

My thanks to James Hadley of Arts Council England London office and the wider Grant for the Arts assessors for helping me to develop my surgery programme and this book, and to Richard McMunn of the Book Publishing Academy for his guidance in bringing this manuscript to Internet and printed life. I recommend him to anyone exploring the world of publishing.

My thanks also to Alan Cranston, Fiona Orr and Kieran Cooper for reading early drafts and to Kate Latham and Alice Newton for their proof-reading recommendations. And continuing errors remain mine.

Many thanks to Gregory Doran for his message of good will – I well remember standing in the dole queue with Greg in Bristol when he suggested that we might work together on a national tour of Romeo & Juliet. We did – and it broke even with a major national sponsor.

I dedicate this book to my grandmother, Gladys Maude Cressey Tozer, who brought me up until I was 10. Nan inspired me to do "stuff" and introduced me to theatre and charity fundraising and event management. I pay immense tribute to my step-father, Peter Tozer, who introduced me to stage lighting with Crawley Operatic Society, to Dorset House School where I did my first front of house and stage work until I was 11, and then to Christ's Hospital school which, helpfully, built a theatre at just the time I needed a new challenge. Balancing school work with company management of school plays, resident stage management and lighting for international touring companies and setting up tours with Julian Garner and the Frog Company all set me on a rather inevitable course. Finally to my mother, Sally Grady, who brought me into this world and after struggling with Alzheimer's for too many years, passed on, leaving some funds to allow time to write this book and to help us all move forward to the next stage of life.

Seven Ages of Man

All the world's a stage,
And all the men and women merely players.
They have their exits and their entrances,
And one man in his time plays many parts,
His acts being seven ages. At first the infant,
Mewling and puking in the nurse's arms.
Then the whining schoolboy with his satchel
And **shining morning face**, creeping like snail
Unwillingly to school. And then **the lover**,
Sighing like furnace, with a woeful ballad
Made to his mistress' eyebrow. Then, a **soldier**,
Full of strange oaths, and bearded like the pard,
Jealous in honor, sudden, and quick in quarrel,
Seeking **the bubble reputation**
Even in the cannon's mouth. And then the **justice**,
In fair round belly with good capon lined,
With eyes severe and beard of formal cut,
Full of **wise saws** and modern instances;
And so he plays his part. The sixth age shifts
Into the lean and **slippered pantaloon**,
With spectacles on nose and pouch on side,
His youthful hose, well saved, a world too wide
For his shrunk shank, and his big, manly voice,
Turning again toward childish treble, pipes
And whistles in his sound. Last scene of all,
That ends this strange, eventful history,
Is **second childishness** and mere oblivion,
Sans teeth, sans eyes, sans taste, sans everything.

William Shakespeare, *As You Like It*

Aspiring/Emerging

Mewling & Puking: the infant creative artist

It was my pleasure to work with Second year students at Mountview Academy of Theatre Arts www.mountview.org.uk in 2012/13. There is nothing more fascinating than working through a programme of skill-sharing which helps an actor (or any creative artist) to prepare for their start in the profession.

So without insulting anyone, let's treat this as the "Mewling and Puking" stage of creative practice. Whether you have previous experience or are straight out of school, when you arrive at drama school you are putting your trust in a group of teachers to support you, and allow you to find your first tentative steps in the world.

At the end of the book there is a section of A-Z (p132) for those thinking of going into drama school or to formal training. It's in the Second childhood section if only because, to be a success in the arts you have to still love to play. Then you need skill, business sense, hard work and a load of luck.

I worked closely with Rebecca Jewell as we fashioned the newly-created Industry Liaison Office, and here, in brief, are a few of the suggestions we made to our cohorts of actors, technicians and directors.

Who do you know?

Who were you at school with who went off into a sensible job? Don't lose touch with them; keep up to speed with them on Facebook; make them into a section of your contacts database. In time, they may have the gift of "time, talent or treasure" to offer you. (Much more on why these contacts are important, and "time, talent or treasure" later in this book.)

Who have you been taught, lectured or directed by? Make a list of every person who has seen you work (even if you don't think they noticed you in a group). Use some form of database (Excel is fine) so you can track their name or what they do by type. Are they mainly a director, voice coach, workshop leader, casting person, or agent? You may not even have their full name or any contact details at the moment. Don't worry – get down whatever information you can. This is going to become a goldmine for you later. You may not know when, but at some time the fact that you can write, honestly, to someone and say "You may not remember me, but you inspired me in x class, I wonder whether…(whatever you need)". This is therefore a warm-call not a cold-call.

Which theatres do you know – especially out of London? Think of your hometown, other areas where relatives live, other nations you have connections to. Make a list as another tab on your Excel list. Why do you know them – have you performed there as a student, or seen a show there? Do you know the name of the director of the theatre, or one of the permanent team? More rich information for you to hoard away or to share.

Don't rely on your memory. If you've never done something like this and you are now Mewling that no-one told you when you were in training – don't despair. Start now.

Who have you seen whose work you admire? Each person's list is different. BUT IT SHOULD BE A LIST. What work have you seen by them, where, when? Maybe a hyperlink to a review you agree with, or a website or a photo to jog your memory. Keep programmes and cast sheets.

Work with some buddies

You can't research the whole profession by yourself. You can't know the whole of the UK geography and theatres. But if you are at drama school, then you are in a class of highly knowledgeable people. You could keep everything you know secret just in case one of them overhears something you know. Or you could join together as a group and share information. Who do you know who knows loads about Manchester? Who has been to/lived in Edinburgh and understands a bit about its creative scene in and out of festival time? Who is fantastic at researching useful blogs because they love it? Who reads *The Stage* each week and can share what they pick out?

If you are reading this and you are without an instant buddy network, make one. Find 4 friends to create a researching/supporting cell of 5 people. You don't have to like the same things. In fact it is best if you have wide interests. If one of the group is an avid soap follower – brilliant – they can think storylines, casting directors, and lighting design credits for all of you. Meet once a month for coffee or chamomile tea. Have a short formal agenda. Share what each of you hopes to achieve in contacts in the next month. Keep in touch and support each other.

The first one of your buddies to get a great job – give an almighty cheer. It's fantastic news. They are on the inside and able to feed new information back to you. Plus they can buy the next round of coffee. Don't do the jealous/mooching around thing I have heard tell happens in some schools/ gatherings.

A group of independent producers who are all sole traders working from home have formed something called SOUP thebestsoupintown.tumblr.com and they gather every few weeks for just that – soup and sharing ideas – pain, suffering and joy. It stands for Some Of Us Producers.

Have a business card

I really think it works. You are out with friends, seeing a show, leaning against a bar. You chat to someone and they want to know more about you. Or you want someone to send you some information about a show, event, or themselves. What better way than to have a simple card giving your contact details and profession? They cost peanuts. You can get a new one done as your career progresses. But don't wait until you have the perfect 10×8, or the best address, or the new website – get started now.

As well as your main residence, if you happen to have a parental home/living accommodation elsewhere, and you really want to work in that nation or region, then put it on your card.

Make sure you have a sensible email address. Fluffykins@ hotmail.com will not make me feel confident that this actress has the depth to play Juliet, even if you are perfect casting. Change it. Re-route it. Then get the good one on your business card.

So your card might look as follows:

Fred Bloggs

Currently Training: Mountview Academy of Theatre Arts

Actor/Puppet Maker/Clarinet

London and Scotland

fredbloggs@gmail.com 07713 644444

website or Spotlight or LinkedIn or site where more info available…if you have one

---

This suggests that you are serious about your profession, studying at a recognised academy and that you have two very special additional skills. I suggest you don't overkill with a long list, and also only put on the card real things that make you stand out from the crowd. You are available to audition for work in the South East and also work in Scotland. I can find you by email and mobile. Sorted.

You might add a photograph – your call. I tend to have different opinions when asked that question depending on the person asking. If you are likely to get offered work partly for your looks (ie. an actor rather than a lighting designer) then fair enough. If you think your look is more memorable than your name (any profession) then great.

But whatever you do. Just do it. Get a card. Get your email sorted. Have a mobile with a clear voicemail message on it.

Clean up your act

If you've had a rather wonderful student life, with many parties, and lots of friends taking snaps of you when maybe you were not showing your best side, then go to your Facebook page. Pretend to be a casting director (or your dream employer) and work through your site slowly and methodically.

Get rid of crazy photos.

Make sure it's up to date with roles played and details of your life experiences so far (same goes for LinkedIn or your own website).

If you are a composer and somewhere in your laptop you have some great tunes – find a place to get them up there for the world to see. If you juggle, make sure there is a great picture of you with fire sticks juggling your heart out. If you look great in a kilt get a picture up there (if you don't look good in a kilt – take the picture down).

Don't lie on your site. You will be found out. And that's true of everything about you and your self-promotion. If you've never been on a horse, don't say proficient horse rider.

Develop your skills

If you can't drive – think about learning. They say you will never be cast in a cop drama being filmed sitting in a stationary car unless you can drive.

If you can't swim – learn – no-one will cast you in an Edwardian punting scene unless you can swim...even if the pool is 6cm deep.

If you once played the piano and stopped – start again. Just get your muscle memory back in gear again.

If you've always wanted to play saxophone – now's the

time to barter some lessons with people. It's never too late.

Think of all the skills that you have and make sure they are as good as they can possibly be. You are simply expanding your employment possibilities.

Get another career

I don't mean to sound depressing, but almost everyone in the arts, from actors to directors, from writers to marketing people, sometimes has to earn a living doing something else as well.

I have been suggesting to drama schools for years that one 3-year degree course available should be joint honours. You spend half your time learning your creative skills, and the other half getting your City and Guilds in Plumbing or another practical craft. You will then never be out of work.

You might take a year off from slogging around the acting or directing circuit to travel and write a book. Then you could make your wages up by connecting across all the country with your Excel goldmine of theatre contacts and offering your building or decorating skills to pay the bills.

Working behind a bar can be soul-destroying. The trick with the "other job" is to find one which takes up the minimum amount of time for the maximum pay, and that allows for flexibility and freedom.

So if you are currently in the Mewling

Key Points:

and Puking phase – think what you could learn in parallel to your main training, and don't miss out on money making/life-saving opportunities.

Two real examples – we have a great actor friend who we have turned to for some great house painting. He's reliable, understands our crazy lives, comes to stay for a few days in the house, charges very reasonable rates – and does a great job.

And secondly – I missed out on helping to set up and run, what was to become, a very successful regional and West End production company when I was 21. A good colleague was setting up the company and wanted me to be his Administrator. A fantastic opportunity. He had decided to fund the production side of his business by buying up old property in Leeds, renovating them, and selling or renting them out. He was a great carpenter. He needed a mate. DIY is not my strong point so I passed up the opportunity. Chris joined up with Jon and they had 10 amazing years putting on shows on tour and into London. They had a couple of hits. They made money and they lost money. But they kept the business afloat by being able to sidetrack their careers, when needed, into the building trade.

Make one or more CVs

Your CV will change all the time. You may have many variations. You may reduce your plumbing ability in one CV, and highlight your love of Musical Theatre in another. Never just send a standard CV to a new contact without reading through first. Try and personalise the covering email or letter to highlight something that would interest the reader. Help us to see you as a standout, interesting, and interested person.

See loads of stuff

Whatever your creative craft, the more you see, the more you will learn. Keep a notebook with you at all times and write about what you are seeing. If you are a lighting designer then don't just focus on the lights, but think about costume, and the play as a vehicle for your art.

If you've seen a great performance don't feel shy about saying thank you (see networking below). If it's a fringe show, stay at the bar, wait for the creatives to come out. Talk to them.

See Readings and Scratch Nights, Fringe shows and major stuff, tiny pop-up exhibitions and massive blockbusters. It may be good. It may be uninspiring. But it will always give you an experience to add to your knowledge base.

Look outside your world

If you love Shakespeare – then make sure you go to loads of other events and shows as well. Be inspired by everything you see. Read voraciously. Use your time to look into things you don't know, don't understand, or are skeptical about.

When someone mentions they are going to see the crop circles in Wiltshire, or to the latest political rally, or look after egg shells in their father's collection, or learn Morris Dancing – you don't need to go with them, or share in their passion. But have a quick look at what they do; open your eyes to the most extraordinary world out there. Don't be blinkered. In 20 years time you may be asked to use all 4 extraordinary experiences in a single production.

[Prize to anyone who can email me a legitimate play, opera or musical which could rely on the leading actor/designer/ director understanding crop circles, egg shells, politics and Morris Dancing. I look forward to hearing from you.]

Meet people from other worlds

You want to (or are) working in the creative industries – that is "exotic" to many people, and completely beyond reason to others. It's very easy to stay with your own clan, and reach the end of training with a wonderful close-knit set of actor/designer friends, and not a single friend who is a yoga teacher, bank manager, investor, travel writer, property owner, etc. But if you cultivate a broad circle of friends (see old school list above) then you can bring your "exotic" life to meet their potentially interesting or even desirable worlds.

Get fit

It's easy to stay in the pub with mates after training, or collapse in bed with a good movie. We all need to relax of course. But don't hibernate. In my classes at Anglia Ruskin University where I taught Arts Management, I asked each week "what else have you done with your creative week?" and too often, at least half the group couldn't think of anything. They had worked, read, been shopping, but they had not tried to expand their brains or get mentally fit for the life ahead. They'd probably walked past and ignored the local museum, the library, the gym, the theatre, the pub with live cabaret and jazz, the poster of a free reading of new poetry. Try something new.

Network

Through all this period of Mewling and Puking you should be honing your Networking skills.

Here are a couple of Blogs which cover the areas of Networking, and getting over yourself.

BLOG 130220

How do you have the nerve to....?

I've just done a drop-in session for 20 third-year acting students who are about to open in *Spend Spend Spend* at the Cockpit Theatre (26th Feb – 2nd Mar). This followed a day of teaching about the ecology of the arts across the UK. (What is the Arts Council? Why do some producing houses get six times the Arts Council funding of another, for what appears the same amount of work? Who might employ actors in Cumbria or Manchester or Eastbourne?) My day also included meeting two trainee technicians also about to embark on their careers.

How do you have the nerve to...put yourself out there and sell yourself, network, find or make work, get noticed? It's a scary process for anyone trying to enter any profession, but maybe most for a profession where each job is likely to last a matter of weeks, and then you are once again unemployed and facing the prospect of selling yourself yet again.

One person I met absolutely inspired me. Ben decided he wanted to get some work experience in theme park technical theatre. He thought Disney. He had GCSE French. He had three weeks off over Christmas, so how to get a job in Disneyland Paris? He didn't know anyone. He looked up the name of the Chief Executive. He wrote to them. They were new to the job. They passed the letter direct to the head of entertainment. That person saw the chutzpah of my colleague. He got a three-week placement in Paris and made, from what I can understand, a very good impression. Brilliant.

Now that takes nerve... but so does walking into an audition room, or going for an interview, or talking to a stranger at a party. But you have to gather your nerves, and your skill, and do it. My wife runs a course called The Art of Being Heard for the business world, bringing these skills to the attention of workers and managers of every age, experience, and level of be-suitedness. I try to bring the same support to every emerging creative I meet. Once in a while I meet a Ben and go – "Good on you for taking a chance."

Three things people should remember. A) The person interviewing/auditioning you is desperate for you to be good/brilliant/perfect for the role – then they can stop sitting behind a desk and get on with their life. B) People you meet love to talk about themselves. If you find them interesting, they will in turn be more interested in you. C) Almost everything to do with presence and calmness begins with good breathing. Before entering a room, take a moment, breathe deeply, calm yourself, believe in yourself and go for it.

And if you are networking (or in a party situation) there's a difference between "stalking" and being noticed. Stillness, listening, being interested are brilliant skills to practice.

Good luck Ben with the next stage of your career. "Break a Leg"/"Merde" to all those showing their skills in *Spend Spend Spend*. And remember that we as agents, producers, employers, and audience members want you to be good (and believe you will be).

[Editor Note – as I do the final proof, June 2014, I am told that Ben Phelps has just won the 2014 National Stage Management Awards – GDS student achievement award. Brilliant News]

BLOG 120309

Making connections...just do it!!

This is a short challenge for anyone wanting to move forward in the arts business, as an administrator, a producer, a creative (for those who like to differentiate between admin and creative), actor, singer, dancer, or even commentator.

I hear far too often the wailing of individuals..."I don't know anyone", "my agent isn't getting me a job", "Mr/Mrs Big won't be interested in me." Instead the individual sits at home, goes to the pub, goes to the movies, and waits for the phone to call. I challenge you to Make Connections...Just Do It.

Yesterday I spent £8 to have the privilege of meeting the Chief Associate Director of the RSC, [*Book Update: Greg Doran – now Artistic Director of RSC*] and a Voice Coach of the RSC with a group of RSC actors.

[Edit note – the eagle-eyed amongst you will note that I have known Greg Doran in the past and so my finding him in a crowded room and going up to him may seem a cheat. But I was only one of a number of people who used this opportunity to introduce themselves – and so can you. So imagine I didn't know him for the purposes of this Blog extract]

Not a bad investment to make to meet two of the most important people in classical theatre today. How did I get an audience so cheaply? Who do I know? What's my method? I will tell you the secret. I heard a rumour that they were together on a panel talking about language and the Bible. I was in Stratford seeing the extraordinarily sexy *"Song of Songs"* created by Struan Leslie, Head of the RSC Movement Department. [*Book Update: Currently freelance after changes at the RSC*]

I had made a connection that no amount of cold letter writing, or waiting for your agent to sort a meeting, or emailing could achieve. I was standing face to face with two major talents of the RSC.

I walked to the box office and said, "I gather Greg Doran is doing a talk about something, somewhere in Stratford, tonight...can I get a ticket?" They sold me a ticket. I was making connections.

The talk was fascinating, they were both stunningly eloquent, and I learned loads. And at the end of the talk I went up to the platform (as did a number of the audience) and said "thank you, you were inspiring, you were great", etc.

Another example from 30 years ago. ABSA (now Arts and Business) were doing a roadshow around the UK talking about raising sponsorship and linking to the business community. I was a student at Bristol, trying to raise money for our theatre company, the British Universities Shakespeare Company, to produce a tour of *Romeo and Juliet*. I went to the talk (free). There were around 75 people there from all walks of the South

West Arts sectors. It was a good talk. Mary Allen from Mobil Oil (later Arts Council, Royal Opera House, and High Tide Festival) talked sense about making the right pitch to business. At the end she, and her colleague panellist said – "any questions, do come and talk to us afterwards." I did. No-one else did. (PS I was scared witless...get over it.) I asked an inane question of Ms Allen, and she was interested in what I was doing. She offered to meet with me sometime if I was in London and talk more about the project and the challenge.

She didn't sponsor us, but she was immensely helpful, and in the end we found sponsorship from ICL (a computer company). I continued to gain good advice from her for 3-4 years afterwards. The reason she was so interested is because, she told me, Bristol was Day 6 of the road show, and she had made the offer every day, and I was the first person to come down to the front and ask for help. Just Do It.

She had made the offer every day, and I was the first person to come down to the front and ask for help.

Just Do It.

I offer one bit of advice all the time to emerging creative colleagues – and it's always the same. You probably know many people (by name and reputation if not yet personally) who could give you good advice and maybe help directly. Find where they hang out. Go and see their work. Go to their talks. Read their books and go to signings. Tell them you admire them/their work (that's the special ingredient!!) and then ask for their advice. Don't ask for a job, don't drop your portfolio or 10x8 photo in their beer, don't stalk them, don't interrupt a private conversation – but just introduce yourself and be interested in them. They may just be interested in you.

Three things to do this week:	Tick when Done:

Three things to set up for ongoing Practice:	Set A Date to Start

Three things I can feel good about that I've done already	Congratulations... time to become a Student of the real world.

PS – when you "tick" something off a list – try using a highlighter pen to mark it as done, rather than crossing it out. All the things you have done will shine out at you.

Shining Morning Face – out in the big wide world

At whatever stage of life you may be, there will be a time when you enter a new workplace and feel that you are a student again. It may be a new job, joining a new creative company, starting a new creative project, joining a Board. Or maybe you are, indeed, just graduated and about to try to find your way in the big wide world.

Let's, for a moment, presume you are wondering how to get noticed, where to be to get noticed, and how to hook up with the right people. And indeed to start with the biggest question – who do I need to be noticed by...or should I say **By whom do I need to be noticed?**

Let's presume for the moment that you may have a little difficulty with the phrase "Putting it out to the Universe" or "Constructing your own reality." So what practical steps could you take to emerge from your Mewling and Puking learning phase, to richer, targeted research?

You can't be everywhere and do everything. In marketing speak you need to "narrowcast" rather than "broadcast" – no one has the time or the money to hit every possible target. So you need to be strategic.

The 3 advert game as a first step:

What would happen if you opened your morning paper, turned on your radio/TV channel of choice, or logged onto your most useful websites and apps – and there in front of you were three adverts which made your heart race and your brain whir. These three adverts are each perfect for you. They are crying out for you to apply. Indeed they are really only asking you, personally, to give them a call and satisfy their need. Each is different. Each is starting at the right time, in the right place, with the right people, for the right money, and with the perfect need for your skills. That would be quite a day. Now don't blow it…

Take a pen (or flex your key-fingers) and write those three ads. (There may only be one. There may be two. There may be four – but no more.)

Be very specific as to what you want to happen NOW in your career. If you are an actor straight out of Mountview then "Director of the National Theatre" is not quite what I had in mind.

[Although "a goal is only a dream with a deadline" Napoleon Hill. So if that is your goal…set a date. A realistic date. And work towards it.]

If you haven't got paper with you – use the back of one of your business cards. If you haven't got a pen with you, GET ONE NOW. If you haven't got a notepad (old fashioned with paper) then get one. If you are totally digital – fine – but back it up.

Each advert should excite you. It should feel realistic but a bit of a stretch. But it should help you to focus on what you really want to do next.

It could be a great advert for the perfect, flexible "other career" which gives you the space and time to write, create, study more, work for free, make your own company. It could be someone wanting you to start a company or make something happen from scratch. It could be a quick project/job. It could be your life's calling.

Now. Take one advert and, preferably with a buddy (see below) dig into the advert.

Which company wants you to work for them? – what do you know about them? Who do you know there? Who's on your excel sheet (see above)? What work have you seen of theirs? When could you visit and see them (I don't mean stalk them…just visit a show, an event)?

Where is the company, geographically? – Do you know someone you could stay with near there? What place do they play in the community that you could learn more about?

What skills do you need to fine-tune? – what does the advert ask for? What else might they need? What would impress them?

Lots of questions, all designed to help you focus on narrowcast marketing.

I was recruiting for staff once and had my favourite (bad) answer to the question I posed at one interview (for an arts management paid trainee) which was as follows:

Me: Why do you want this job?
Him: It's close to the bus stop.

That may be true, but it didn't get him the job. If he had been able to say that he liked what we did or maybe he'd been to see a show (or even that he'd wanted to, because his mates had, but he couldn't afford it). Maybe if he'd said he would be excited to work with us because then he'd get to see Queen live in concert, or Welsh National Opera, or even Jim Davidson in pantomime. Then he might have got himself the job – which only required that he showed a sense of wanting to work with us.

So you have your adverts. Maybe they will change as you think more. Maybe you will ditch one of them. But this is a starting point to focus your attention on where your future research, arts attendance, and general passion could be focused.

Don't just sit in a darkened room and do this. When you have your three adverts, tell your friends. Take time to think about each place and each job. Go out there and look for those adverts. Be aware.

And be positive about it. These are your three perfect jobs/projects. Believe that you are right for them. Make yourself better at the things that might trip you up at interview or audition. Focus your CV to meet the jobs. Go out there, believing that you will make this happen – and something extraordinary may just happen.

PS – let me know when this exercise works for you. It worked for me. Ask and I will tell!!

Let's take an example: "I'm an actor. I want to work at the RSC." That's my positive advert.

But I can't afford to go to see their shows, and I'd never get to meet the directors, and, and, and …excuses excuses.

Let's presume (as I always do in CGO Surgeries) that you are as good, if not better, than you say you are. So here are a couple of Blogs which suggest ways to reach your possible goal. Read them and do some translation to your own artform, creative hotspot, and life plan.

BLOG 130509

Unique performances of Shakespeare at the RSC…for a fiver !!

There is a wonderful opportunity available to all audiences to see one-off, adrenalin-fuelled, unique performances of the Shakespeare canon in the RSC theatres. I was there this week for *As You Like It* and I will be back next week for *Hamlet*. Historically, these performances are held behind closed doors, and now, fantastically, they are open to the general public. They are understudy runs.

I declare an interest. My son, under his equity name of Michael Grady-Hall, is playing Silvius, the shepherd in the main run of the production directed by Maria Aberg in the main house. This week, he gave his rendition of Touchstone the fool to a packed house in a performance he may never have the chance to give again, presuming the brilliantly engaging Nicholas Tennant remains healthy for the rest of the run in Stratford and Newcastle. However Michael, like all the other understudies, is now ready to step into the role at a moment's notice and that is great.

The joy of these performances is that they are slightly anarchic and unexpected – not least because, to misquote Jaques, one man in his run plays many parts. And this week David Fishley must be crowned as man of the match. In this one lunchtime performance he played 5 different roles with a show-stopping moment as Duke Senior, saddened to witness the hunger and exhaustion of old retainer Adam in the arms of Orsino. Although to deliver Adam's response, he had to jump swiftly into Orsino's arms because he was not only playing the upright Duke, but also the languishing retainer. A leap which brought the house down; a moment to relish for ever.

So next week I'm heading back to Stratford and again seeing the full company, led by Jonathan Slinger, giving us their *Hamlet* and then, on Thursday 16th at 1pm I will return to the play and see a unique gathering of actors giving us a full scale, fully staged version of the production but with a very different cast. I can't wait.

So as an aspiring actor, designer, writer, theatre producer, agent, photographer, visual artist – just think how for a fiver and an advance train fare from home, you could have used this event (as well as enjoyed the show).

Here's a space just for you to think about it: and if you don't want to help yourself to any of these rich pickings, then think of a Buddy who may not have thought about the RSC yet – and doesn't know what's available for a fiver.

To hammer home the point…and to float an idea buried in this Blog which might inspire someone to pick up on an old Grady idea – here's another RSC for a fiver blog.

> **Using this opportunity:**

BLOG 120501

A crowd of RSC understudies

I'm not sure what the collective noun for understudies are…a crowd, a break maybe, or an opportunity of understudies. Anyway today I had the pleasure of seeing a whole cast of understudies giving us *King John* at the Swan Theatre for the RSC. I was there, as part of a proud extended family, for actress Mariam Bell who gave not only an immensely powerful Constance but also her dirty dancing Blanche – and indeed at one point, both together on stage in conversation.

It's normally a privilege only for those involved with the productions, and those who are friends of friends, to see the understudy runs, but this performance was also open to the public, and so there was a goodly audience of normal theatregoers seeing the play and the production for the first time.

It was a really fine cast of actors, getting their only chance to give a full understudy performance of the play, and giving us, and the RSC casting department, agents, and members of the rest of the RSC company of actors, a chance to see each player in a different (or two different) roles. They are a fit and healthy group of actors unlikely to go sick, and so for most it will be their only chance to play these leading roles, and our only chance to see them. Until, that is, they themselves get cast in future productions of the overall repertoire.

I was particularly delighted to listen to Assistant Director, Sophie Ivatts, giving a warm-up and mini-masterclass on the role of the understudy and the process of preparation of these roles. She explored the dilemma between making the role personal to the individual performer, yet able to fit seamlessly into the original production, and honouring the original intentions of the lead actor that they are understudying. A balancing act which every cast, Assistant Director and originating director has to tackle. I most definitely enjoyed, to quote Michael Boyd, the "mad inventiveness of an RSC understudy run."

Twenty years ago I suggested to the Society of London Theatre that they might create, with a couple of us as producers, a touring Sunday night musical project – gather a cast of understudies of the principal roles of each of the musicals, create an ever-changing show which was itself a celebration of the shows playing in the West End, and then tour it to those theatres across England where there might be audiences who would decide, having seen the show, to go into London to see the full production. The idea was not of any interest to SOLT then – but I just thought about it again and so float it again.

[With no interest from SOLT, a producer and I created for Buxton Opera House a show entitled *Wonderful West End*. After a successful first tour, the producer bought us out and it toured for 10 years. I think it was the first of many subsequent songs from the shows. But still I think a SOLT official show, with a classy marketing and group sales operation, could do wonders.]

Two things strike me as I re-read this:

(1)   Always credit anyone you see whenever talking about them. Don't just say Andrew Lloyd Webber's *Sunset Boulevard*...take a moment to acknowledge the lyric writers, the book writer and maybe even the orchestrator, without whom the piece would not be ready, on the page, for the director to direct and the designer to design.

(2)   Think of writing a Blog or reviews of shows and things you have seen. Even if it has limited readership, it hones your writing skills, and gives you wonderful memories of creative work done and witnessed.

One of my bugbears about the industry, maybe mainly Musical Theatre, but I sense across other artforms too, is the failure to cheer new writers and leading artists. We need to celebrate the stars of tomorrow before they become stars. See (1) above and the blog below:

BLOG 101220

Unsung writers

How do we cheer new writers if the existing ones remain unsung?

Am I alone in being concerned to hear repeated time after time "Cameron Mackintosh's new musical *Betty Blue Eyes*". It is brilliant that Cameron is getting this musical onto the West End stage, but there needs to be a balance between using Cameron as a brilliant marketing and producing guru (which he is) and honouring the creative talent which chose to take Alan Bennett's work and steer it through to a fully-fledged musical... I hope that he is also working with his marketing team to ensure that the names of George Stiles and Anthony Drewe are remembered way after the hullabaloo of opening night.

I have quite often been asked to give my "state of the musical" address to emerging writers and producers hankering after the limelight. It invariably starts by considering the world pre– and post-*Cats*. Cameron harnessed a great energy in 1981. He took a massive risk and it paid off. He may not have invented the reproducible musical, but he made the art of reproduction a masterclass in creativity and commercial acumen. Books, essays, thesis projects and speeches have since been written and presented. He created (or at least harnessed) a phenomenon, made even greater in its impact through his tireless attention to detail on his own personal shows for 25 years. His is a masterclass in marketing and creativity – and I have had the privilege to work with him and know that the art matters absolutely to him, in every detail.

However his success also led to three things that have restricted the creative release of the next generation.

First, had *Cats*, *Les Misérables* and *Phantom* been fantastic hits and run for 5-6 years, the young Cameron would have been driving forward to find, nurture, and commission the next great musicals to replace them. He'd have been in his 40s and he'd have helped to find a wealth of new talent at that time. One problem (in my personal hindsight) is that he and his productions were worldwide phenomena. The energy was spent on the creation of productions around the world of these very works. The theatres were filled with CML productions. Twenty years later they are still filling the theatres. One result is that there are very few producers in their 40s and 50s supporting and commissioning new work, because Cameron and others of his generation (Bill Kenwright, the Lloyd Webber empire) have hit rich seams of work which have kept the theatres filled.

Secondly, Cameron and others began to use the logo as their primary marketing tool. It wasn't Claire Moore in *Cats*. It was "the eyes." Interestingly, when the show started, the cast were engaged to be announced in alphabetical order. However, as the marketing kicked in this was changed and Wayne Sleep and others were highlighted. Good marketing reasons – they could help to sell tickets on an unknown show. Now 25 years later, there are very few stars who have been chaperoned through live Musical Theatre to become marketable household names. A whole generation of 30-50 year old performers who have played the great roles in the blockbusters are unknown to anyone but the ardent collectors.

Thirdly, the sheer success these major "now and forever" shows have together generated a thirst for a massive emotional blockbuster. They have popularised "event theatre", where the public say, "I don't go to theatre, but I did see *Phantom*."

The mass audience for Musical Theatre is wonderful, but the assumption that this audience is there for something different from audiences that go to theatre, opera or ballet does the art-form a dis-service. I am not suggesting that what Cameron and others have done is not fantastic for the business of theatre, but it does have its knock-on effects. In the 70s and 80s there was a place for dramatic Musical Theatre alongside dramatic plays. Now the drama of film and theatre has exploded onto our screens and stages – we are wanting and willing to experiment. But for Musical Theatre writers, there are few chances to take risks, because there are few opportunities for new work to come to a commercial or major audience base.

And without taking risks and having opportunities to try out new work, and fail, and try again, then new writers may not get to be the best that they can be.

What I am writing here is, thank god, in danger of becoming a null-and-void historical footnote. The Musical Theatre business is changing. Perfect Pitch has taken over from the destroyed Vivian Ellis Prize. The Edinburgh Festival new Musical Theatre works scene is rich with work encouraged by the MTM Musical Theatre Awards. Musical Theatre Matters MTM [now renamed Musical Theatre Network] and Mercury Musical Development MMD are hard at work creating new opportunities. The major reps and producing houses from the National to the RSC, the Bush to the Traverse are working with Musical Theatre as part of their rich tapestry. And the Arts Council of England includes Musical Theatre in their art-form listing for the first time since its inception. That's all great stuff.

This blog is written to plead, politely, with those who can make a difference at the very top of the production tree and to those designing their very first posters and promotions:

a) Please acknowledge and champion the writers you are working with

b) Please cheer and credit (on posters) the top performers you are engaging

c) Please nurture the next generation of producers – and don't sideline them.

I so look forward to seeing the rich tapestry of Musical Theatre in the future – when the Arts Council, the regional theatres, the fringe producers, the emerging West End, and the established master producers are all exploring the next generation of writers, performers, and creative talent – and giving it due credit for its creative involvement in this most extraordinary of art-forms.

To George and Ants – I hope *Betty Blue Eyes* is a fantastic success for you, to rival *Honk!* across the world.

[Edit note – as I write this June 2014 *Betty* has had a highly praised re-imagining and opening at Colchester Mercury thanks again to the phenomenal determination of Cameron to make his shows have a long and healthy life. It is now on a national UK tour.]

Back to the plot.

You have your adverts (p19). You have focused your attention on 1,2,3 opportunities and now you are ready to get out there with your "Shining Morning Face" and make connections.

Edinburgh for shining morning faces

For many creative artists the place to go to meet people and find connections is a festival. Whatever your art-form there is one. And if you aren't sure, then sure as eggs is eggs, your art-form will be represented at the Edinburgh Festival. The Festival is in fact 5 different festivals rolled into one – the Book Festival, the Fringe Festival, the International Festival, the Television Festival and the Edinburgh Military Tattoo. Not to mention a gathering of many art galleries into a festival within a festival, the self-styled Comedy Festival within the overall Fringe, and the amazing Free Fringe which has grown within the Fringe to be a wonderful array of events and performers – all for a donation in the hat at the end.

There's something for everyone. There's enough audience to go around [I honestly believe that – at least for the determined professional artists, taking the event very seriously] – But you need to be there with the right show, in the right place, at the right time (of day), with the right image, and with the right way of marketing yourself. And most importantly knowing why you are there, and who you want to have visit your event.

They'll be more about Edinburgh as we go through this book – but for now a few words of advice...[And here I am focusing on the Fringe, where anyone can take a show, rather than the other Festivals which are "curated" and selected for a specialist audience]

a) Go to Edinburgh as a punter before you take a show/risk anything in Edinburgh. It is a different world, playing by different rules, and can be the most miserable place to have a flop event.

b) Don't ever stop learning. If it's your 15th Edinburgh still go to the briefing sessions run by the Fringe, and read any packs produced by your art-form specific advisors.

c) Get loads of advice from Fringe veterans. Listen to the advice of the venue where you might play. Explore all options.

d) Read Mark Fisher's excellent book, *The Edinburgh Fringe Survival Guide*.

e) Study the other shows in your art-form who have been there, done that, had success, had a tough time. Talk to them. Learn from everyone. We are all very generous with our helpful suggestions when it comes to the madness of the Fringe.

Here's a quick Dos and Don'ts which, I think, I wrote with Alison Goldie following a Devoted and Disgruntled session. [If I have taken someone else's great list, my apologies]

Edinburgh or bust!
Dos and don'ts for the Edinburgh Fringe

Do...

Research on sponsors
Target certain audiences/ groups
Talk to people – the Fringe Office, your own company, your venue
Network like there's no tomorrow
See as much other work as you can
Specify everyone's roles within your company
Read a business text to learn what makes a good press release
Socialise
Ask for and respond to constructive criticism
Have a great publicity idea for the Royal Mile
Know how to pitch what you're pitching
Find networks for people in and around your profession/skill base
Be confident

Don't...

Sign contracts without knowing exactly what you are signing up to
Keep your connection a close-knit thing – get to know people in other areas
Book too big a space
Take it personally
Hope it will work out
Get too drunk
Underestimate cost – prepare to be broke
Rent a house with too few beds
Forget to thank everybody

BLOG 081208

Getting noticed – Fringe Sunday & Ben Moor

Dodging rain showers, it was great to see so much fun being had across the Meadows. All the performers' tents seemed packed, and wandering through with my Producer Associate, Tom Atkins, we were musing on what it takes to get noticed on the Fringe. With thousands of people milling around, and hundreds of companies with leaflets, a few obvious things still seem to be missing in terms of preparation.

Earlier in the day I'd spotted a representative of one of our companies looking relatively insignificant on the High Street, in his own clothes, with a few leaflets and badges. He was competing with the likes of *Jet Set Go*, resplendent in their airline uniforms with matching luggage parading down the High Street completely in character and engaging with the audience. On the Meadows there was a really strong presence from Precarious with *The Factory* playing at Zoo Southside – everyone had posters on placards above their heads, they were strategically spread around the grass, you couldn't miss them, and they talked to us. They inspired us with their show. I've booked my ticket. On the other hand there were lines of people silently holding leaflets hoping we might want one. Spot the potential audience member, come up, chat to us, we're there to be interested – otherwise we'd flee the Meadows in an instant.

When you've been performing in Edinburgh for a few years, your face is familiar, it's like seeing an old friend, and that was how I felt in Wk 1 when I spotted Ben Moor just chatting to people by the Fringe office. I was delighted to say hello again, get a badge, and now I have just returned from seeing his show *Not Everything Is Significant* playing daily 3.15pm in the

Pleasance Courtyard. I don't know what it is about Ben and his writing, but it always makes me cry. It is haunting, thoughtful, open hearted; a multilayered flight of fantasy, and a joy to discover. Not surprising Upstairs was packed and he is getting great notices.

I think we are just going into Week 4 of the Festival – or that is I have to admit how it feels a bit today. Actually just starting Week 2 – we've only been playing 11 days – and new companies are arriving and doing their tech rehearsals. *Misterstourworm And The Kelpie's Gift* are settling in to bring Stuart Patterson's magical tale to children and families, David Hertzog delighted us in the Singer's Cafe with selections from *George M Cohen Tonight* which opens tomorrow, and the cast of *Missing Mel* resplendent in matching t-shirts are hitting the Royal Mile to flyer for their Youth Music Theatre (YMT:UK) show which opens on Wednesday. Stan Strickland and his colleagues from Boston have arrived for *Coming Up For Air* – sax intact, bongo drums currently missing in transit. Ahhhh. Each has the tough task of capturing an audience when so much has already opened. If you are coming up to the Festival or reading this blog and have friends in the area – please spread the word.

Now off to see *Perfect Pitch*: a concert of new work in development for 2009 and beyond. And to find the cutting for one of our shows from the weekend – I gather *Miss Saigon* won the pretend Scotsman award for the Show Most Likely to be Sued. All good publicity and gets them noticed.

Now add a few more Do's and Don't to your own Festival List – expanding to a Festival where you might feel excited to create/perform.

> **Do's and don't at festivals**

[Edit – in re-reading this Blog it reminds me to say to all bloggers out there – try and remember to name check as many shows as possible and offer their performance times. You may be writing about one key show, but do name-check a few others where the promotion has impressed you, or you've heard good things. Help to fuel the word of mouth. Thanks]

Just a footnote in this section, to look at one other Festival that are more specific to a particular art-form. High Tide Festival in Halesworth, Suffolk, is a celebration of new playwriting and new playwrights. It is now a 10-day celebration in this small market town. Upwards of 100 actors, directors and creatives settle here to bring amazing new work to life. The homes of West End serious theatregoers, producers and critics are abandoned for a visit to the idyllic county of Suffolk, and the chance to spot hot new writing.

If you aspire, as a shining morning face, to work in new drama then where else would you choose to be for a few days? A colleague of mine is writing his MA dissertation on new writing. He was rushing around by email and train to reach useful people to interview. I suggested an afternoon in the café at the Cut in Halesworth might sort him out. I left him in deep discussion with the dramaturge of the Bush, with a meeting lined up with the director of the High Tide Festival, an offer to meet one of the major West End drama producers for lunch, and the tempting sight of David Hare on one side of the café and the legendary Michael Billington on the other.

The thing about festivals is that important/useful people are away from their desks, in a relaxed mood, propping up a bar or grabbing a sandwich. If they've just done a reading or performance you can tell them they are brilliant. If you are both about to go in to see a new piece of work you can talk about expectations. There is a levelling out that manages to bring you closer to people who could help you. And as I propose many times in this book – most people like to be asked their advice, or engaged with. We all enjoy being inspired by new passion for our specialist subject.

There is so much more to explore for the Shining Morning Faces, but now I move on to the The Lover.

The Lover – with the woeful ballad

This part of the Aspiring section looks at those who are creating work – composers, emerging companies, theatremakers. Those who need to have the work as good as it can be, to impress/involve someone else – a director, a producer, a backer.

I suspect I am talking more to those in the performing arts than the visual arts – but I hope some of the material will be useful to skim through, and make your own variations on any of the suggestions included.

This part of the Seven Ages is split into three sub-sections:

- **What Makes A Hit – and how might you find an amazing idea**

- **Workshopping and improving the work**

- **Being the best you can.**

What Makes A Hit – and how might you find an amazing idea

When I worked at Plymouth Theatre Royal as Head of Marketing back in 1982, I had the pleasure to work with the Artistic Director of the Repertory Company within the theatre, Chris Hayes. He continues to direct widely. He had 10 years running a high quality commercial producing company, and is known to thousands who have gone through RADA short courses as the man who supported them. He taught me a

> Take a moment – what 5 things would you think will make a hit show?:
>
> Now turn the page

massive amount, and together one day, near the end of both our tenures in Plymouth, we wondered "What makes a hit?"

Over the years, I have played with the list a little to reflect my own personal passion for what I call "necessary theatre." But basically, it is the same list I have used in discussions with directors and writers and producers and theatres for 30 years.

Needless to say they, and I, don't always heed the advice of the hit list...or remember to check in time. Have a try yourself with the last few plays/shows you have seen.

The Hayes/Grady Hit-ometer

How many of the following does your show/event/creation have?

Score 4...should be OK. Less...watch out. More...hit material!

1. **Title** – should be known (or at least feel very familiar) to the audience

2. **Star** – actor, or director, building confidence for the audience

3. **Company** – should be known or respected

4. **Uplifting** – I feel that I'm likely to have a positive emotional feeling

5. **Spectacular/Epic/Surprising** – when I see it (or what I hear about it)

6. **Archetypal/Universal** – so that it speaks to the audience deeply

7. **Good** – after all the hard work, the audience must think its good

It's good to have all 7, but I sometimes add another personal one – which is that, as I get older, I really only want to see theatre which I think is "necessary." It in some way touches my heart, gives me a lift, makes me think. I explore Necessary Theatre later in the book (p90).

Here are a couple of examples that Chris and I used to test our theory...after the event:

The opening seasons of the Drum Theatre included: Tom Kempinsky's *Duet for One*, an adaptation of *The Hitchhiker's Guide to the Galaxy*, *Pistols* – a show by Heathcote Williams on the Sex Pistols, and Sondheim/Wheeler's *Sweeney Todd*. [Apologies to the adapter of Hitchhiker – I can't remember the author...or find my programme from 1981]

Let's see how I would score them now:

	Duet for One	Hitchhiker	Pistols	Sweeney
Title	0	1	1 – not the show, but the material	0.5 – it was the first small prod post London.
Star	0	0.5 – one of original series	0.5 – writer	0
Company – all inhouse	0.5 – respected locally	0.5	0.5	0.5
Uplifting	0 – suicidal	1 – crazy fun	1 – power	1 – revenge
Spectacular	0 – one woman in wheel chair	1 – great set and costumes	1 – music	1 – the chair & band
Universal	0 – hope not	0.5	0	0.5
Good	0.5	1 – audience loved it	1 – wild	1 – raved
Totals	**1**	**5.5**	**5**	**4.5**

I'll leave you to guess the lowest and highest box office returns for the season. Which was a shame because all were fine and worthy pieces of theatre to do.

This is very subjective scoring. But then so is creative and artistic programming. So is planning the next piece of work you want to do.

NB – I am not suggesting you choose your own creative project by scoring like this. Far from it. But I am suggesting that, when you have chosen a project, you see whether you could stack the odds a little in your favour with something to bring your hit rating a little higher.

When I moved from Plymouth, via the Edinburgh International Festival, I landed at the Traverse Theatre charged with promoting 7 new plays which were opening between February and July, and then all coming together into a mass repertoire during the Festival. We decided to launch the marketing of all 7 together with a single leaflet and a chance to buy tickets for all 7 at once. This was great for showing the breadth of the work of the creative team, and allowing the audience to plan their theatre-going. The challenge was that some of the writers hadn't written their plays yet. All new work, and all gestating in the heads of the likes of Chris Hannan and Jo Clifford. My 40-word copy for each play had to reflect what I thought the author was trying to say, where the play was not complete or even conceived yet. In the end I got 6 pretty right and 1 spectacularly wrong. Hey ho that's live theatre.

Applying the Hito-meter above for this selection of unknown plays suggests something like the following results in advance sales, without the benefit of having opened to audience or critics:

Titles – unknown and in the main unfamiliar (0), **Star** – a company of actors who were wonderful but not household names yet – Tilda Swinton and Ken Stott were just two of the names who would go on to pack theatres and cinemas and boost TV ratings. Peter Lichtenfels as Artistic Director was known, Jenny Killick and Stephen Unwin as the new associate directors were not yet known to the Traverse audience. This was a first big season for them (0.5). **Company** – the Traverse was and is an important local, national and international player (1). **Uplifting** – unknown plays, unknown subjects, rather sketchy 40 word promotional copy, spun to make them sound as attractive as possible (0.5). **Spectacular** – not in the standard West End way, but design and use of the space for each piece by emerging high quality designers always offered a quality experience (0.5). **Universal/Archetypal** – yes the work of the Traverse usually spoke deeply to its audience, although work unknown (0.5). **Good** – well again, the Traverse audience was loyal and expected the work to be good (0.5).

So my overall score – trying to remember my feelings from early 1985 – is that the season as a whole would have an advance score of 3.5. Then the shows started opening and got fantastic reviews overall. A level of excitement for the season grew. Word of mouth spread. And so the "Good" score and the "Uplifting" and indeed the "Star" scores rose. By the time the Festival season arrived, reviving all the works, the small Traverse Theatre and its Studio space below were packed. A deeply exciting season of which to be a part. And only one of the 7 productions was mis-represented by its 40 words of copy, much to the annoyance of one writer.

Having gathered the best hand of creative cards you can, then there's another stage to this process – and that's being clear who you are aiming your work at.

If you are cast in a play, or helping in a company to create a piece of work – then it is also really good to do this next exercise.

[Edit – I use the following process all the time. Indeed only yesterday (May 2014) I was doing a series of one-on-one CGO Surgeries in Colchester. I met with a post-apocalyptic filmmaker, a dark clown solo performer, a playwright exploring the edges of humanity damaged by society, and a personal business branding specialist. We used the following exercise in each case. It is very effective and very simple.]

ARTICLE FOR AMA – ARTS MARKETING ASSOCIATION 130918

Who do you want on your front row?

An introduction to the basics of marketing your event.

Let's presume that you want a full house when you plan your event, or a packed gallery, a "rush off the shelf" book sale, or a campsite filled with happy festival-folk. This brief introduction is designed to help you go from idea to full house. It's about planning. It's called Marketing.

David Packard of Hewlett Packard is quoted as saying, "Marketing is too important to be left to the marketeers" and whether you have a marketing department, a marketing person, or no dedicated person, everyone who cares about their art, and wishes their event to be witnessed and enjoyed, needs to know about Marketing.

Excuse me for using theatre as my basic example from now on. All other art-form leaders may need to adjust the odd word – but the sentiment is the same. To borrow terms from Open Space (see p114), "Whoever Comes are the Right People",

"Whatever Happens is the Only Thing that Could." Your task is to make sure the "right people" know, and are encouraged to be there and that what "happens" is going to get the desired result in the hearts and minds of the audience. Angela Lanyon, the wonderful theatre manager I worked with at the Theatre Royal Plymouth used to say that my job, as Head of Marketing, was to get the audience in to the theatre, her job along with her front of house teams and the artists on stage was to make them come back.

So back to the basic question. Who do you want on your front row?

Never assume that someone else is going to decide on all of this. Make it your business to think about the answers to this question. It could be something you do in the privacy of your own room, or it might be something you do with your team, your cast, or your community.

So why do it? Very simple. We none of us have enough money to publicise the show or event in every medium to ensure that every person on the planet knows about the show. We want to spend the least possible amount of money and time on getting the message across to the people who will want to come to the show (and those that we'd like to want to come to the show.) That's called target marketing or narrowcast (as opposed to broadcast) marketing.

The strategy should include discussion about **Pricing** (how much can people afford, what do we think it's worth, are there incentives we can make to help fill weaker performances, or attract people who might shy away from the price). Then look at the event (or **Product** in commercial marketing speak). What are you actually hoping to sell? What are the different elements that make up the overall product? If you've chosen

What are you thinking?

this play or event, or you are working on the planning for that event, then you will know more about it than anyone else. What are the selling features which make this event stand out?

Next, have a think about your audience and understand where they live/work/spend time when they might make the decision to come to the event. It's no good splashing publicity all over your venue if there isn't much passing trade. That might feel good for the soul, and impress the staff and the actors – but it isn't going to sell tickets. So think about the **Place** that your marketing message is going to have the maximum impact. That place may be the kitchen table as the customer opens their post. It may be the mobile phone as they check twitter. It may be the school common room as the teachers think of how to inspire their flock. It may be in the 24 local vegetarian restaurants around the town as you try to reach a very specific group of customers. Finally, think about **Promotion**. How are you going to phrase the information, how will you be most persuasive in your message and what medium will you use: print, radio, talks to groups, e-mails?

In marketing jargon, these are the 4 Ps – Price, Product, Place, and Promotion. Too many people muddle up marketing and promotion (or publicity) in the same breath.

They are two different things. The marketing process is the planning and thinking about your customer process. Within the marketing mix, you will then use different forms of promotion and publicity. But think marketing first.

For me the easiest way to start is to ask myself who I would like on the front row. Who are the 5 people (say) who I want to be sure to reach, so that they choose to spend 2 hours in a darkened theatre enraptured by my piece of work? Or they choose to walk up to my gallery and show their delight (and their cash) as they see my exhibition.

I suggest that at the very first stage of planning an event you think of these 5 people. Give them each a name and a backstory. Make sure you know their age range. Make sure you think where they might go to work or play. Think about other shows and entertainment they may also enjoy. Think about their family. Do they buy the ticket? Do they attend the event alone? Are they coming in a group, where another person has planned the trip and booked the coach? Are they brought by a parent or a teacher? Know your 5 key customers. Really know them.

You can see desperation in the eyes and actions of some producers when a show isn't working. Suddenly the mass adverts come out, the new poster, the new offers, the mountains of direct mail letters to anyone who has ever passed their data details. That is broadcast marketing because the narrowcast marketing was either never done, or misfired badly.

If you identify them, then it's much easier to think about the price that they might be able and willing to pay. It's much easier to think of where they might be when they hear about the show and get excited enough to book. It will be much easier to think what elements of the product most appeal to them – and remember each one of the 5 members of your front row may be there for very different reasons. And finally

45

you will then be able to think through the right promotion that will be seen/heard in the right place, excite with the right message, and offer the right price to get them to buy.

Whether I'm talking to a major Brazilian producer about the promotion of a new production of *Miss Saigon*, or working with a new show being created by my wife's Authentic Artist Collective, or thinking who might come to my own CGO Surgeries, I start with the very basic question. Who do we want on the front row?

We don't usually have the time, the luxury, or the money to "test market" our shows. We can't mount a production and play it for a week to see whether our marketing mix is right, and then realise the theatre is empty and shut for a few weeks to change all the publicity material and try again. You can see desperation in the eyes and actions of some producers when a show isn't working. Suddenly the mass adverts come out, the new poster, the new offers, the mountains of direct mail letters to anyone who has ever passed on their data details. That is broadcast marketing, because the narrowcast marketing was either never done, or misfired badly.

I've had my fair share of mis-firing campaigns. I am happy to share the horror stories face to face with anyone. I continue to beat myself up about a few poster images which in hindsight were never going to hit their target. I have written some spectacularly bad copy for a few shows, which completely misread the audience. And I have stood in despair at the back of an auditorium watching a wonderful show with an empty house wondering what I did wrong. I keep learning. One of the problems with live theatre is that you can't always see the finished show (or sometimes even the script or synopsis) before deciding on the 5 audience members and the campaign to reach them. That's life. We didn't choose to work in the arts because it was easy.

So "Whatever Happens is the Only Thing that Could Have", and "Whoever Comes are the Right People." That's the nature of life. The wheels of life will keep on turning. A new challenge will be presented at your door. A new project will need an audience. And there'll be another chance to think of the 5 people who should (or could) be there.

If you are lucky enough to work with an organisation which can build up a mailing list, or you work with an organisation that has a reputation for good work, then there are times when you can mine your existing audience and reputation to fill the house.

You might get 70-90% business just by putting the name of the show on a post-it-note on the front step of the theatre. I guess David Bowie and Kevin Spacey in the National Theatre production of *Play X* directed by Rufus Norris, with all tickets at £10 and featuring some cute donkeys and some winners of *The X Factor*, plus the most amazing cameo from the new Doctor Who would do ok. Maybe you don't need to do much marketing to make that sell.

You may have some time on your hands. How about spending that time doing exactly the same process but with a slight twist? Who would we love to have on the front row who might never have seen our theatre, or realise that we have tickets available and we want them to see our work? Who is not coming to our shows? Who are we excluding just because of our success? And how can we encourage the next generation?

Every time I start a new job, or work with a new artist I ask the same question. I love talking to a couple of successful

Who would we love to have on the front row who might never have seen our theatre, or realise that we have tickets available and we want them to see our work?

Who is not coming to our shows? Who are we excluding just because of our success? And how can we encourage the next generation?

(or stuck) creative artists who have never thought about marketing. I love the challenge, just occasionally, of trying to talk about narrowcast marketing with those who think marketing is something done by the lowest of the low, just one step up the ladder from the box office staff. And I love having that conversation with the staff of a box office – because they know their audience, often personally. They are talking to them every day.

To marketing departments everywhere, I urge you to get away from the desk, away from the email, away from the office and go to talk to potential audiences, and look at current audiences, and talk to those who work with audiences. Statistics, databases, print schedules, press copywriting are all wonderful tools of the trade – but first and foremost get to know just 5 people in your front row.

Workshopping and improving the work

I'm invited to loads of workshops, showcases, and productions of new work. I've been lucky enough to be there when some very fine works start as a few songs and a synopsis. I've also despaired when I see a show that someone has spent hundreds/thousands of pounds/ dollars on presenting to me and others – and a 10 minute conversation, or a couple of songs on CD, or a couple of scenes sent through to a mentor, or development specialist would have resulted in the same reaction – either this is not for me, or even worse this is just not good or ready yet.

Here is a blog that suggests my path for a work. See if it works for you, and if it doesn't think through your own path.

But please don't start preparing the work with a first night invitation. Start with the art and ensure this lover is never creating a "woeful ballad."

BLOG 130425

Scratching can make it better

I've had a wonderful theatrical and celebratory 13th anniversary weekend with my partner Kath Burlinson. Between us, we have run an amazing workshop, seen 18 short films from the PG Mountview Students, done 7.5 hours of yoga, seen 3 professional theatre productions, and held an inspiring CGO Surgery. Plus a Sunday walk and a latte or two. I will leave those who know us to decide who did what.

But my blog focus is on a subject that Heather (independent producer) and I explored in our recent CGO Surgery – the path of a new work from commission to acclaim through all its possible stages of development. And the need not to muddle up the different stages. I think there are five very distinct stages for a new piece to be fit-for-purpose and it is fun for WhatsonStage readers to think, as they see a show, whether they agree with my segmentation, and whether a particular show has gone through some or all of the phases. I'm specifically thinking about new writing.

Can I in passing recommend everyone to visit The Shed at the National Theatre and see *The Table* – a wonderful smorgasbord of ideas exploring many generations of family and relationships, phenomenally performed, and for me very very emotionally powerful (but then, like one character, I missed my father's death having only met him once in life... another story).

49

The Table had been through much time in the amazing National Theatre Studio. Theatr Temoin's *Ninevah* which we saw at Riverside is powerfully gathered through two years of collaboration. Both passionately offered to the WhatsonStage reader and general public after going through phases of development.

So my five phases – after the initial writing team has prepared a first draft, Heather and I talked of the **Table Reading**. A time for the writer to hear their work off the page for the first time, offered to them by first-rate, sight-reading actors (or singers if it's a musical). In private, with only the closest allies present (no backers, no possible producers, no public, no family and friends). Around the table read the play, then take a break and then sit with the actors and explore the piece – writers are amazed at the perception of any actor for their own character. It's all the actor cares about and so they have immense focus. The writer needs to be strong to receive comments like "why is my character doing this?" "why am I not aware of what x or y is doing?" etc.

[Edit – I interrupt the flow of this blog with an idea I was exploring with a writer yesterday in Colchester at a CGO Surgery. My thanks to coach Rachael Stevens for this idea I've played with. Instead of sitting round the table and talking with the actors, you as a writer might experiment with turning your back on them. Take a chair and settle down with your back to the table. Take a notebook with you and say nothing. Allow the actors to talk about the play and have a discussion amongst themselves around the table – maybe facilitated by a colleague or just free flow. Let them talk passionately, openly, critically, supportively. You remain silent. Just listen and take notes on what you hear, what resonates with you, what feels useful. Let the rest wash over you. Then when they've finished and you've got all you can from their conversation, turn around and re-join them, close the process, and have a large swig of your favourite drink. This process offers the table readers more freedom, and you a rather privileged position of hearing what you want to hear. Try it and let me know if it helps. Now back to the blog]

The writer then heads back to the keyboard (or the pen and ink) and develops the play further, leading slowly to the next stage when they have a piece that feels ready for further exploration. Welcome to **The Workshop**. Here the writer steps away and hands the piece to a director and actors for a few days. The writer isn't present. The actors and directors come up with ways to help the piece move forward. The writer comes in after a few days to see what has happened – the writer can take away anything and everything. They can ignore or use what they have heard. This also works for musicals, when the composer should not be at the piano, indeed should not be in the room until the sharing.

The workshop is for the writer. It is not designed to lead to a showing to anyone else. Again, this is a private developmental process.

Along the way between workshop and showcase, many creators enter part of the work into a **Scratch Night**. There are many variations, and inventive names to match, but essentially it's a chance for "knowing" audiences of theatre folk and friends to watch 3, 4 or more different pieces in one evening and then feed back comments to the creatives in the bar afterwards or in formal discussions. It's a chance for the writers to see what a random audience might think of the idea, and test out elements of the creativity. It's usually a press-free event and can be immensely supportive. It's also great fun to go to – so check out your local theatre, to see when they are scratching a new work. If they don't have such a date in their programme, why not suggest it to them? – there is so much new work out there that deserves to be seen, and maybe you could help create a scratch night.

If you are preparing for a scratch then choose the very best material, gather the best actors/presenters (not your mates who need a job) and concentrate with your creative colleagues on making this 5-10 minutes really count. You don't know who will be in the audience. Don't try out material that you feel is shaky – you are making an impression and you don't know whether a possible producer or champion may be in the house. If there is a feedback session, or the chance of a questionnaire on the seats, then think carefully what feedback you need. Shape some questions that could help you on the next stage of the journey.

If for some reason you want to show some material which may be shaky, then tell the scratch audience before and invite us to enter your world and understand why you may be presenting something which fails to ignite/excite us. Don't just leave us guessing. Set us up properly.

And next comes **The Showcase** – too often muddled with the workshop. This is a sales event. A chance to take the best bits and show them off to producers, money people, theatres, tour bookers, the star you want to excite, and your most supportive colleagues. The cast and creatives who gather to present a showcase should know their material, be confident that they are presenting the best work, and be on the same page as the writer. It doesn't need to be the whole show – I've seen fantastic showcases of First halves where a character walks down at the end and simply says "if you want to know what happens next you'll need to back a full production...thanks for joining us...see you in the bar." I've seen hit songs and wonderful narrated set pieces, all designed to whet my appetite (or more usually unlock a cheque book) to help get the piece seen.

And finally, if there is no rush to book the show and take it into a major production, then a **Skeletal Production** can help. Bare bones, little set, simple costumes, first class cast (often on profit share or low rates – but be careful to comply with the best guidelines and practice for payment of artists...everyone has to eat), presented with highest professional creativity in a space that is going to attract the right people to be sitting in the audience. A new musical for a week at the Landor Theatre will get the Landor Musical Theatre audiences coming to check it out. A special new play at the Finborough Theatre on a series of Sunday/Monday nights will get the Finborough audience to explore the new work. Each house has its specialism and will reach its mailing list and online audience followers quickly and easily. They'll take a chance on a new work and see what happens. Then you have a few weeks to get the piece seen and excite producers, maybe with a run in Edinburgh or at the Oxford or Buxton Fringe Festivals. Maybe a small tour you create yourself.

So that's my 5 phases of development. There are many variations – but when you, dear Whatsonstage reader, decide to go out of the West End to see a new work, check the programme, talk to the creatives in the bar, and understand the process that has gone into creating the work you see. It's often a labour of love, and your enjoyment (and maybe even your contacts) could help the piece move further.

At whatever stage of development you are, remember The Show Must Go On (if at all possible). Back in Edinburgh at the 2008 Festival, here are two examples of good decisions made by the Producers.

BLOG 080801

Where 2 or 200 are gathered together – let the show go on

There were two great lessons yesterday on the first preview day – they both relate to the very simple adage that "the show must go on". The producers and everyone involved with *Only The Brave* were in a great state of concern after the only dress rehearsal of the show. It is an immensely complex process bringing an orchestra, a full cast, and a technical team together and they were concerned that they just weren't ready for the public. We were expecting 200+ people arriving at the theatre and, quite reasonably, the producers were in debate until the last minute. In the end adrenalin kicked in, the show happened, the audience was buzzing at the end. Everyone acknowledged that the show was infinitely better than the dress (as often happens). Now the work of shaping and tightening the show's presentation and sound will happen and audiences will, I hope, be delighted by the sheer passion and power of the piece. A bit like jumping off a cliff for all concerned – but they proved they can fly.

The other wonderful lesson of yesterday came from producer Arianna Knapp of SenovvA Theatricals and writer/performer Maggie Simpson. Their production of *Queen Of Wyoming* didn't have any advance sales for the first preview, so it could have been a chance for a rest or a bit of private rehearsal. Not a bit of it. Arianna rustled up a few of our staff who were on break and instructed our stage managers of George 2 to leave the doors wide open, so that passing strangers could hear Maggie performing and be welcomed in if they chose to pop their head around the door. The show went ahead; within minutes there was a decent group of people watching. Just after the show,

I had a text message from one of the most important group sales and promotional men in British theatre to say "thanks" for *Queen Of Wyoming* – he'd had a great time. A perfect lesson on "the show must go on". Now word of mouth will start spreading.

Day 2 of the first festival of musicals: songs from Parade can be heard in the Singers Café, preparations are underway for the first Cabaret evening here. *Cannibal* and *Greyfriars Twisted Tales* are preparing for the first previews of their world-stage-premieres. (By the way, Kopperberg Summer Fruits cider is fast becoming a hit with my team.)

Returning to the Seven Ages – Lovers need all the help that they can get to be the best lovers that they can. They need great partners, great parties, and lovely opportunities to learn technique. That's true of Producers too…and both young lovers and emerging producers may be extremely hot.

Here is a quick plea to any Wise Ones and Soldiers out there – people who you know who have positions of importance and could help:

BLOG 130301

Emerging producers are poor – can you help ?

At my surgery on Saturday at the National I was talking with one emerging producer and we realised that one of her problems is that she cannot afford to see all the work she would like to. She is restricted in the main to the National Theatre (thank you Travelex and Under 26 schemes) and the Fringe. She rarely sees West End work or the work of the major London producing houses. She is not an actor or a musician, and so she misses out on Equity and MU rates. She is not part of the ticket agency circuit or a friend of the right "guest lists", and so rarely gets the special offers that flow around the place. I was reminded of a scheme I set up 15 years ago with West End producers. I wonder whether there's a way of getting it started here – but this time for emerging creatives.

When I set up and ran New Musicals Alliance (now part of Mercury Musical Development) I had a deal going with all the major Musical Theatre producers (bar one) – and I wonder whether anyone would be willing to create it again. Each member had a voucher, and if they wanted to see/study a West End show they could go to the box office at 7.29pm and the deal was very simple – if there was an empty seat in the house they could sit in it for free. If there was some restriction that made "free" impossible then they would be offered the lowest possible discount that anyone could get at that performance.

In this way a writer (and now a producer) could go 2-3-4 times to see a major show, and study it carefully. See different casts. See different musical directors at work. Consider the show from different parts of the house. All designed, 15 years ago, to make the writer a better writer. If any producers are reading this, they could give young producers and creatives the chance to study your work in depth, without being either rich or knowing someone influential. This could be immensely easy to run regionally as well as for those based in London. A complete sell out with no no-shows is a real rarity for any theatre.

Any producers, networks, marketing agencies, or angels interested in helping make something like this happen? Plenty more ideas where this one came from – just give me a shout and see whether CGO can make connections.

Let's stay with the Producer for a moment, or anyone creating new work. At an Open Space Technology session (see later) I had time to think of the common problems, and how the Surgery programme has helped to unlock some ideas.

I offer the notes from that meeting here and strongly recommend any creative being, especially those working in creating theatre with its widest spectrum, to look into Open Space and the annual major Devoted and Disgruntled event run by Improbable for theatre practitioners. It's in London for three days in January. But anytime of the year you can log onto the D&D site and explore over 600 minutes from individual meetings which have happened over a number of years.

Here are just some of my notes from one of those sessions:

OPEN SPACE MINUTES / 2013

What are the challenges for a producer & how do CGO Surgeries explore them?

I called this session for a discussion, but it also served the purpose of being a one-on-one for 2-3 creatives present at Open Space..."Whatever Happens..." Initially I had 10 minutes to myself and so I sought to take time to focus on the issues which often come up, and which we can often solve, in a Surgery:

As an emerging producer or creative maker of art, there seem to be 5 fundamental and deeply linked questions:

Where do I find...

a) Money

b) Venues and collaborators
c) Artists and creatives
d) Projects or Co-creatives
e) The right audience, paying the right price, in the right numbers

In each case I start with the same basic premise – my guest at the Surgery knows far more than they think they do...

a) Money

If you need to raise money then, unless you are going for mega bucks, the first task is to list colleague theatre folk (who may know people), school friends (who were sensible enough to go into another business), family (who may support a fringe or small creation), local and connected businesses (think laterally with some colleagues), specialist trusts and those who work in the field your show might be exploring, your own college or place of business, and finally, very finally, the Arts Council.

b) Venues and collaborators

Go for the ideal – think location and venue that's perfect for the project. Think who might be excited to partner. Again who do you know who knows someone?

c) Artists and creatives

Don't presume the dream team is working – they may well be out of work or just wanting some new inspiration. Think very specifically about the project, then expand to include all those you admire, and maybe also linked to the venue of your choice.

d) Creatives

Think of all those who have ever taught you, inspired you, or are the very perfect people for this project. The web is wonderful – you can find an email or at least where they are working very quickly. Don't stalk them, but do follow them and see whether they can be inspired by your "elevator pitch."

And **e) Audiences** – we covered in other sections above in this book.

In CGO sessions we work together to make lists, make timelines, and work out how to free up your own time so that it is effective and efficiently used.

After I made my notes, I was then joined by Eve, Ros, Sheena, Pamela and here are some thoughts which were added to a list. As I said, there are hundreds of minutes like this available on the D&D website. Here was our list:

- A mentor is so useful
- See how Stage One can help
- There are 800 young directors on the Young Vic Theatre scheme
- Old Vic New Voices
- Think regional networks and if there isn't one, start one
- The challenge is to be respected for your work as a producer (and ££ valued – see excellent session on fees). Beware spending too much time supporting people with cups of coffee when you could be making work. There's a balance.
- How can/should ITC respond to the fabulous growth in creative producers
- Can the Arts Council nurture this growth, maybe with listings and site

- Could there be a site for short term/practical work projects with ££ which creative producers could hook into to earn some money.

This is a short list – and general to the people present at the time. There are wonderful books to help, such as James Seabright's *So You Want* to be a Theatre Producer? And then there is a blank sheet of paper, a mentor, and your own brain. Together they make powerful connections.

Finally, in this section, may I add a few thoughts on the need to shine at every performance offered. To be present in every moment, and whatever your age or experience, to be the very best that you can be.

Being the best you can

BLOG 130204

What makes a fantastic performance / Taboo and Second circle

Last week I went back to see the new company in *Taboo* at the Brixton Clubhouse, my third visit. The first two were on behalf of the show's worldwide representatives on earth, Stage Entertainment Licensed Productions, and this time with colleagues from Mountview Academy of Theatre. In this case we were there to cheer Paul Treacy who has taken over the role of Boy George even before he'd graduated from Mountview. He is wonderful and a joy to watch. He has just found an agent, and I suspect we will be seeing a lot more of Paul in years to come. If you get the chance before March, do try and see this cast (or this amazing, outrageous show for the first time if you haven't already seen it).

It's quite edgy, and the master of ceremonies enters into some pretty dangerous territory as he talks to the audience. I hadn't expected the rest of the audience (or indeed my Mountview colleagues) to learn quite so much about Kath and my life together...but the MC asked, and she told him!

Patsy Rodenburg www.patsyrodenburg.com has explored this phenomenon extensively in her book *Presence* – she talks of First, Second and Third circles – introvert/wishing you weren't there/non-connecting in First circle, extrovert/self-absorbed/not listening/not connecting in Third circle, and finally balancing power, vulnerability, passion, listening, and presence in Second circle.

What made Paul Baker as Philip Sallon (and the MC) so appealing was his total connection with the audience. He saw us, he challenged us, he connected with us, he listened to the energy of the room, and then delivered an award-winning performance. When he gives us his massive ballad "Petrified" in the Second half, the pain and humanity shone through to us. I couldn't believe he had ever sung those words before, let alone that he has been delivering this phenomenal performance since preview 1 of this production.

Patsy Rodenburg www.patsyrodenburg.com has explored this phenomenon extensively in her book *Presence* – she talks of First, Second and Third circles – introvert/wishing you weren't there/non-connecting in First circle, extrovert/self-absorbed/not listening/not connecting in Third circle, and finally balancing power, vulnerability, passion, listening, and presence in Second circle. So thank you Paul Baker (and indeed the young Paul Treacy) for being in Second circle for us.

I had reason to expand on Ms Rodenberg's basics with the Second Year Mountview acting students when we were exploring choosing their headshots for Spotlight. Also exploring how they would get over the insecurity of meeting agents and doing the networking which they all know they will have to do. I recommended they all read *Presence*, and think how being in Second circle can be associated even with a photo. They have to find a photo for their CV which is going to show their inner soul, and somehow speak to the agent, casting director, director or producer about the real person behind the 10x8.

With *A Chorus Line* recently back on our stages with its references to "resumé well honed", it is important that actors understand that a performance like Paul Baker's is possible night after night after night if they understand what it means to be in Second circle. And remember this as a business leader, or job applicant, or staff member, or volunteer, or even someone trying to get served at a bar – being in Second circle gets you noticed.

Enjoy Taboo (but maybe stay in First circle if you don't want your presence in the audience to be noticed!!)

By the way – try Second circle for yourself in unexpected situations. Next time you are at a crowded bar, settle yourself in Second circle. Reach out with your breath and gaze to one bar person. Connect with them. And be very calm. It is amazing how the bar person will notice you and come to get your order ahead of the hidden flowers (First circle) or bolshy pushers (Third circle).

Conclusion – Aspiring/Emerging

...At first the infant,
Mewling and puking in the nurse's arms.
Then the whining schoolboy with his satchel
And **shining morning face**, creeping like snail
Unwillingly to school. And then **the lover**,
Sighing like furnace, with a woeful ballad
Made to his mistress' eyebrow.

Throughout this first 1/3 of this book, I have tried to focus on the time when we are learning, trying things out, beginning the creative process.

If I were to gather 10 key points into a shortlist it would read:

1. Who Do You Know? – you know more people than you think.

2. Network – especially outside your normal world

3. Understand the 3 Advert Game (p19)

4. Say thank you, give credit, cheer fellow creatives

5. Beware of (but look seriously at) Edinburgh

6. Stack the odds in your favour – use the Hito-meter (p38)

7. Understand "narrowcast" marketing & basic marketing

8. Scratch at the right time...make the best work you can

9. The show must go on

10. Be Present/understand Second circle – even at the bar (p61)

   Now...time to grow up

Inspired/Overwhelmed

The Soldier – seeking the bubble reputation

The first section of this book sought to give support, ideas, and practical help to those who are at the start of their career, or setting off on a new journey. Now I turn my attention to the serving creative soldier. You may have fought a few battles, or may be feeling a bit overwhelmed by projects or ideas. You have more battles to fight, new ideas to explore, and a career ahead of you before you can hang up your sword and have a mug of chamomile tea.

There are three standard reasons a Soldier chooses to come to a CGO Surgery. Either he/she has a whole list of projects and needs to work out how to put them all into practice – usually all at once. Or they have done a lot on the fringes of where they believe they could/should be, and they want the world to notice them, and honour them for the creative being that they are. Or they have a single inspiring idea and want some very practical help with taking the next step.

Take A Moment to Reflect

"Stand still. The trees ahead and the bushes beside you are not lost.
Wherever you are is called Here,
And you must treat it as a powerful stranger,
Must ask permission to know it and be known.
The forest breathes. Listen. It answers,
I have made this place around you,
If you leave it, you may come back again, saying Here.
No two trees are the same to Raven.
No two branches are the same to Wren.
If what a tree or a branch does is lost on you
Then you are surely lost.
Stand still. The forest knows where you are.
You must let it find you."

David Wagoner "Lost"

Let's start with the person with a whole heap of projects and explore for a moment what may be stopping them from getting started. It is usually a mix of three things that they don't have enough of – **Time**, **Treasure**, and **Talent**. These are often the three things used to discuss people's ability to support a charity or a Board. For now, let's look at each in turn.

TIME – Often we are running at great speed to stand still. We have spread ourselves too thinly, making ends meet by earning money doing anything but the creative projects we dream of putting into place. We are then doing profit-share, unpaid, or speculative projects that take time and divert us away from the project.

The guidance which I was given, about a year ago, by the excellent Coach and arts manager Rachael Stevens, helped me to shape my last year of freelance life by doing the following:

a) Separate in your planning, the time needed to earn a living from the time needed to make your creative projects come to life.

b) Think how much you need to bank every month to survive, and try to work out how little time you could spend earning that amount of money. (This is where having the plumbing skills, or the computer website design skills, or the music teaching ability come into their own.)

c) Divide your month, or your week into time to earn "to live" and time to earn "to create" your projects.

d) Set aside some of the project time to thinking time, and some to doing time, and some to down time for pleasure.

e) Think when you are at your most alert and creative –
are you a morning person or a late night person?
Choose the best times to do the creative project work.

Now, if you have a full-time job being creative (or work full-time on something else), then finding time for your projects will be more of a challenge. But it is still possible to refocus non-work time into creative time.

If you work in an office, there is a growing habit of eating at your desk, or not taking breaks. Change that habit. Take a break. Mark it in your diary as a meeting WITH YOURSELF. Walk away from your desk. Take your notebook and go away from the office. Even for 30 minutes. Use this time to plan your projects.

If you work freelance, it is so easy to be doing everything at once and never taking time for yourself. Open your diary now and look ahead to find the next available week where you have two days without meetings in them, not together, just two days in a 7-day period. Then mark one of them off now as PROJECT MEETING with yourself. That still leaves the other day in the week to fill with meetings. [Please do it. Do look at your diary. Do try it.]

Somehow you need to carve time out for yourself. And if you are useless at organising your time, then find a friend to help. Someone who might need a talent you have to offer.

> What's The Point:
> "We are all meant to shine, as children do…It is not just in some of us; it is in everyone. And as we let our own light shine, we unconsciously give other people permission to do the same. As we are liberated from our own fear, our presence automatically liberates others."
>
> Marianne Williamson,
> A Return to Love

Don't overwhelm yourself – the aim is to have Time to Think.

There are wonderful Coaches out there who can take you through the process of sorting your own Goals and Priorities and personal expectations. Fundamentally, it is about giving yourself some "me time" to allow yourself to think about projects.

[Edit – I wrote this section many months before deciding to train with The Coaching Academy as a Personal Performance and a Small Business Coach. I'm enjoying working with pre-diploma clients and offering them the kind of support that Rachael offered me.]

TREASURE – A pile of ideas and no money is often the challenge. You dream of a project or a pile of projects, but they are likely to be "best kept secrets" unless you can find funding, investors, donors, and ££$$.

Out there, if the project is good enough, there is funding. There are a lot of people with a lot of money out there. Most of them are not working in the creative industry. They have day jobs and responsibilities and boring lives. You can often seem exotic and unusual to them. But you need to be out there looking for those connections and those networks.

If you have addressed the Time challenge, and freed up a bit of time when you can be working on the speculative creation of some of your projects, without earning a penny to pay the mortgage for a while – then use the time wisely to explore finding Treasure.

Treasure might come from one of 5 sources:

1.   Arts Council/Funding Agency – writing a grant application, understanding the criteria and your project perfectly, trying to get a meeting with the right person to help you shape the application (see Open Space notes here) and then going through every hoop meticulously, applying maybe once, maybe twice, or maybe even three times (as I did to get support for the CGO Surgery programme). It can feel a bit soul-destroying, but in the end persistence can mean your project is funded eventually.

OPEN SPACE NOTES FROM DEVOTED ® DISGRUNTLED JANUARY 2013

Can't we meet the bank manager?

This short session at D&D was inspired by the sense of frustration which I feel sometimes, that Arts Council England's GFTA system is so paperwork driven, that creative conversations and relationship building is more difficult to achieve now than it may have been in the past.

Although the system is clearly created for maximum access and maximum fairness, there also comes a time when the document seems to leave the influence and hands of the arts officers who know the artform and potential project well. It moves to a team who are scoring based only on what they understand from the document submitted. There might be a danger that the skill of getting GFTA grants seems sometimes to rest more with the ability to create a phenomenally good tick-box scoring application, and less about the understanding of the need locally/regionally for the project.

In calling this session I wanted to make it very clear this is not an ACE bash – far from it – but rather "a wondering." A wondering whether there are benefits to be had with the "knowing your bank manager" system which used to work on the High Street to help people get their business going, and whether there were advantages to more opportunities for relationship growing.

Thoughts which flowed when others joined this session:

- Arts Council cuts have seriously reduced personnel and therefore the time to talk.

- A good relationship manager is really important (several of us have great experiences of really good supportive, knowledgeable people with whom we have been able to shape projects).

- An NPO (National Portfolio Organisation) needs a champion in the relationship manager, and someone who really understands the funding system (plus our art-form and aspirations).

- Moving away from ACE we talked about Sponsors – and once again the relationship between the arts organisation and the sponsor is enhanced enormously if the relationship between two individuals is good.

- Interesting example of a sponsor who reflected that. They worried that the arts organisation didn't have any crisis, or shouting, or "help me" moments and so the sponsor didn't get so involved with what was going on. Actually they quite relished a bit of a crisis with another sponsored client because they could get more involved, and help to solve it. So maybe there is again a lesson to be learned – involve the individual in a sponsoring company in the rough and tumble of an arts organisation – they might relish the chance to help.

- We talked also about Trusts and Foundations, and the need to find any way possible to connect with the Trustees, or the officers who serve the Trustees – help them to feel the art which they may be supporting, and understand the artistic vision. In this way it's easier to have a two-way discussion to ensure the art matches the wishes of the Trustees.

A shared feeling through the short discussion was of the need to make all the process as human/connected as possible, whilst also protecting against any accusation or sense of funding only going to people who know people in high places. There's a balance needed for the good of all parties.

2.   Donations – Here we have the advantage of a whole heap of great fundraising sites which can be used as the collecting and the promoting vehicles for gathering donations. Just Giving, Indiegogo etc are there to focus a small campaign. We have Facebook and Twitter to spread the word about our project and the existence of a campaign. But the truth is that however much you hope for hundreds of strangers to support your project, it is likely, in the main, to be supported by people you know, or by people who know people you know.

In Aspiring/Emerging earlier, I suggested keeping an Excel spreadsheet of people you had met. The other spreadsheet needs to be all those people you know who are NOTHING TO DO WITH THE ARTS. People you were at school with who went into banking, or soliciting, or doctoring. Sensible people who are now paying off their mortgage, still working, still commuting, still time-poor, but maybe, just maybe, cash-rich and interested in helping create your project.

If you are reading this before you have a pile of projects ready to go – that's great. Now's the perfect time to use some of your available "research" time to build your Facebook friends, or checking back through the old school album – anything to gather a list of people who might get the first whiff of your project and be willing to help.

3.   Trusts and Foundations – There are the usual suspects. The massive trusts with dedicated assessors, on-line guidelines and helpful websites. Begin to build awareness of these trusts, and see whom they support and the projects, or types of artforms, that they favour. They change their priorities. Keep alert.

The way to track Foundations that support the arts is through collecting intelligence. Remember that all the major organisations that receive grant support and donations will acknowledge them on their websites, or on giant plaques in the foyer, or in programmes: an easy list to start with.

But then there are the unpublicised Trusts and Foundations which may be perfect for you or your project. They may be locally managed by a solicitor or accountant in your town (befriend all of them...see Networking/4N below). They may be connected to a Guild or a Church or a local business or a local dignitary. Knowing your area and building relations outside your own field of arts and creatives will be really helpful here.

4.   Sponsors – Again there are the usual suspects, well publicised through their support of our major institutions, but then there are other companies that may not be part of Arts and Business (the network that that excites businesses to support the arts). They may be local, or have a specific interest in the area of work you do, or young people, or a particular nation where you are doing performances or collaborations.

The trick through all this is to think laterally, prepare to be surprised, and have your business card ready. Three quick examples:

When I was a student, Greg Doran and I started the **British Universities Shakespeare Company** and decided we'd raise £25,000 (in 1977 this was a lot of money...it still is) and tour *Romeo and Juliet* with a company drawn from 14 different universities across the UK. I did something everyone says doesn't work. I made a list of 250 companies. I rang each one and found the name of someone working in the marketing department, or the Managing Director. I then sent them all a pack we had photocopied and a covering letter. We got some lovely "no" letters and lots of "return-to-sender" packs, because I'd got the address wrong.

We had a beautiful simple folder with carefully designed sheets. We had a couple of great names as patrons – because we'd approached some amazing people we didn't know and asked them. Out of 100+ individuals about 8 said yes. Thank you Lord Birkett and others.

We had one approach from a business. A UK major company that had offered limited arts sponsorship in the past. We met a senior Director and he sponsored us. Although in fact, it was a little more complicated than that.

I met the gentleman for dinner in a hotel in Bristol, where he had an office and we had our base. A pleasant dinner exploring the idea. He then asked me up to his suite to discuss the figures. I thought nothing of it. He, however, had realised that Romeo and Juliet is a play which requires a cast of 20ish agile men who will be sword fighting and looking great in tights (oh and a few women to complete the cast). He liked that idea.

He didn't get the kind of return he'd hoped for. Lots more stories to tell. But we did our tour and we were immensely grateful to this major company for their funding. To say thank you at the end of the tour the whole company took him out for dinner. He had centre place at the table. On one side of him was Juliet. On the other side of him was Lady Capulet. Opposite him were our female company manager, our Lady

Montague, and the Nurse. He was surrounded by lovely ladies. The array of males in the company were arranged at either end of the table. Not, perhaps, his preferred seating pattern.

The moral of this story? Each business and business leader has a particular reason why sponsoring your project could be right for them. Not all are immediately obvious. Sometimes, cold calling and mass mailing does land a result. Although I would always suggest researched targeted pitches are preferable.

Another example for you...

In 1988 I was running Buxton Opera House and hatched the idea of creating the very first Festival of Musical Theatre and a global search for new musicals. I first had a year in negotiation with the Daily Telegraph, their Manchester senior players, and their advertising agency. All went well and everyone loved the potential of this global project until it was eventually scuppered, following a scheduled meeting with the Editor in London (fantastic). He was ill on the day of the meeting and his Secretary "depped" for him (OK, PA's are the next most powerful to meet). Only then did we realise that she loathed Musicals. End of meeting. End of a year of gentle wooing. My thanks to the wonderful opera critic, Michael Kennedy, for championing the project all the way. Thanks too go to the MP and writer, Gerald Kaufman, for writing a major feature about the project in the Guardian.

But you can't get round a PA – not even with a rousing song.

Then, I struck lucky. We were holding an occasional gathering for business leaders in the region. A short reception hosted by the Duke of Devonshire, our Patron, then some wine and into a performance of a new musical destined for the West End – *The Windsors* – and then drinks in the interval.

As the guests were mingling around the potted palms at the interval reception, I overheard one say to the other that they were auditioning for *Fiddler on the Roof* at the weekend. My ears pricked up. Musicals. It turned out that this guest was himself "depping" for another colleague who couldn't be there. He was passionate about Musicals. He was company secretary of British Nuclear Fuels. He was interested by the Festival idea but passed it to his Marketing, PR, and Advertising teams to consider. He was not going to make the decision, but if they approved the idea then he would be delighted. They did. He was. The Festival of Musicals took place with Principal Sponsor BNFL for £100,000 in Spring 1992. They also helped us reach other North West businesses to raise a further £75,000 and in the end we got £5000 from the Arts Council.

The lesson of this story – eavesdrop wherever you are! Keep creating opportunities for business networking and delighting business leaders with your art. And then have a cast-iron case for the importance of your project when you need it.

BLOG 120331

Risky Business – arts or investments?

I go to quite a lot of networking breakfasts around East Anglia. It's good for connections, although very bad for the waistline...but I do it for my art, of course. What is fun is that I almost always find someone with whom, at first, I have little connection, but with whom – after a little work – we can find a common ground position, and I can celebrate the Theatre Royal Bury St Edmunds.

This week I was at the Bury 4N (for networking) group (and for anyone who likes meeting fascinating people who could help their business, and vice versa, I would recommend 4N). I was standing next to two healthy besuited 6'2" 40-year-old investment brokers. I was the small, older, fluffy, not-suited oddity in the room. And I challenged them that my business was more risky than theirs...within a moment of consideration they agreed.

The Arts, especially regional presenting, producing, and mixed programme theatres, is/are notoriously risky. The downside is terrible (losing your shirt, job, etc) and the upside is negligible (not much profit if breakeven is 75% and you hope and pray for 80% business). Add to that, the fact that we present at the Theatre Royal, say, 250 risky things a year – every one is different, you can't do trial runs, and there's never really a repeat. OK, we produce plays, but is a new adaptation of Jane Austen's *Mansfield Park* (opening Sept 2012) similar as a "product" to a national touring actor muso-drama about an Essex rapist, *Dick Turpin* which played the same slot last year. Not that similar I think.

I was sharing my business challenges with these two investment managers and, despite the millions of pounds of your money they may play with, they said – it's madness, we make 3 really risky decisions a year, and we can test them if we get them slightly wrong. You make 250 risky decisions, for little or no profitable outcome, and every decision is for a different product.

We talked more, and what was fun was that the two be-suited gentlemen increased their interest in the arts 10 fold, because they started to understand our business as a professional challenge. We don't call our biz "show business" for nothing.

So, if you are an investment banker, financier, or just a normal grown-up business person – think twice about the arts being created by a fluffy load of crazies, and just wonder whether there's something in the fact that we have to balance our books with most of the profitable cards removed from the pack. We often run buildings, with a large part-time/volunteer/paid staff, we rely on high volume sales with low mark-up, and you can never sell the product 1/2 price after its sell-by-date.

If you're a struggling arts manager (or one of the 7 arts managers who is not struggling) then think about the joy you can give a be-suited business manager by challenging them to a game of risk.

[Edit note – I've just rejoined 4N www.4networking.biz and also the Business Scene in London www.business-scene.com/event/london-connections and I recommend both for building connections where you are. Its not hard sell as some of the networks are. Its not closed shop or secretive or single sex. Its about interested and interesting people from a wealth of business sectors coming together to see how they can help each other. If you work in the arts you tend to be immediately slightly exotic and interesting]

5.   Investment – Here you honestly believe that your project can make money. You have figures to prove it. You need money to risk in the venture, but there is a realistic chance that the investor can get their whole investment back, and make a profit.

If you have a project like this, then you need to gather other people's investment documents to be your guide. In theatre you can register to receive investment documents for the West End with the Society of London Theatre. Ask other producers and commercial agencies to give you copies. Talk to solicitors who specialise in arts and cultural investment. Find any opportunity to go to seminars or talks offered by your own trade body or network.

Once again, like donors, you are likely to know the people who will invest in your project. Keep the individual stakes/units low enough and make it very clear that this is a risky venture and it is possible (maybe probable) that they will lose all their investment. Then you need to draft a document, take it through a Solicitor to be within the law, and follow the guidelines very carefully. BUT it is a chance to be part of the project in a small way, and your non-arts business friends might enjoy a flutter.

"Social innovators…are fiercely visionary and hopeful even while determinedly grounding their actions in the **cold heaven** of daily reality testing.

For them hell is not failing; hell is *delusion*. Hell is kidding yourself about what's going on, for therein are the seeds of failure sown. In its essence developmental evaluation is about learning what works, acknowledging what doesn't work, and learning to tell the difference – with none of the blaming of cold heaven attached."

Frances Westley *et al,*
Getting To Maybe

I've only invested in three projects, because I don't have money to lose. I once gathered a group of my school friends and put £300 (I think) split between 6 of us into the West End play *Shut Your Eyes and Think of England*, produced by John Gale. We got our money back and a little bit more. The next opportunity I had was to invest in a new musical called *Cats*. I didn't have £250 available, because I was working at Bristol Hippodrome as House Manager – no spare cash. A little later, I invested in a friend's production of *Hancock's Last Half Hour* and lost the lot at the Boulevard Theatre behind Raymond's Revuebar. A few years ago I was asked to invest in another friend's production. This time it was the London premier of *Honk!* by Stiles and Drewe. I was delighted to help with £100 I think. And even more delighted when I got £75 of that investment back. It didn't break even, but it did pretty well and I felt a part of the production.

I have outlined 5, but there are probably many more forms of "Treasure" to support you in unlocking projects that you want to create.

TALENT – and here I don't mean you are not talented, but you may need partners and people in your team to make the project happen. It's good to be as aware as possible of your own skill set and then to see where you need help. You can't be good at everything – and you benefit from collaboration.

Since you are now an experienced Soldier you will, hopefully, know yourself quite well. There are many systems for knowing yourself and seeing how best you could work in a team. For example, I'm a "2" on the Enneagram Scale. I'm a "Counsellor Idealist – INFJ" according to Myers Briggs. I'm a "Plant" or a "Chair" according to Belbin and I'm an "Expressive" according to Bolton & Bolton. Oh and I'm Virgo. Each and every one of these systems seeks to help you understand yourself and how you relate to other people.

The talent you need around you – if you have many projects and many things to achieve – all need to understand their roles and be supportive. This does not need to cost masses of Treasure or Time, if it is well organised and people know their place. You could creatre a barter system, where you are the expert one person needs, and in return they are the expert you need.

Kill each team member

One trick I used when I have run organisations or assessed group structures like a Board is to undertake a very simple piece of self-assessment.

Working Together

How do social transformations begin? How do social innovators connect to possibility? And how might genuine social innovation be supported?

a) Support **visionaries**: people with a strong sense of calling and emergent possibilities…rather than fall under the enchantment of measurable outcomes.

b) Support **intense interactions**: networking an information exchange among those who have the potential to tip a system in a new direction.

c) Remove barriers to in-novation. Social innovators don't look to government to make things happen. Social innovators make things hap-pen. Social innovators worry about overcoming regulatory and policy barriers that sup-port the status quo, impose controls and sap energy.

d) Speak passionately about the things that really matter to you. Give voice to those you serve who live the problems you want to attack.

$\rightarrow$

I look at the whole team, Board, staff structure and then, one by one, I consider what would happen if they suddenly ceased to exist. I mentally kill off each person. After a moment of grieving, there are one of three things which you realise would happen.

Either – you would try and find someone exactly the same in every respect to fulfil the job. They are a perfect fit.

Or – you realise they are irreplaceable with one person and you would need to split the job and appoint two or more people with different skills to fulfil the roles that this person took. They are invaluable, probably overworked, and they offer a risk to the organisation simply because of their irreplaceability.

Or finally – you realise that you wouldn't replace the person because you could probably do a slight re-organisation and their work could be done by others. Even worse, you may realise that, sad though it may be to grieve their parting, you really don't need to do anything at all because the team will work better without them. This is a place in your organisational review where you need to act…and not let it continue.

So if you already have a Board, or a gathering of allies, or staff, try the Killing Game quietly and see what happens.

Time Talent Treasure – now prioritising

So having explored gaining some more Time for your project, the necessary Talent that you need, and considered the Treasure that might be necessary – the next step is prioritising the projects.

You cannot do everything all at once, and one of the things we have to do with our team is consider each project individually and see where to start. Here a Mentor or Coach can be immensely helpful.

You might try the 3 Advert Game and see which of the projects is first to be the focus of an advert. You might try to create a Gannt chart for all the projects and see how you could create a timeline which got more than one project off the ground.

What is a Gantt chart?

A Gantt chart, commonly used in project management, is one of the most popular and useful ways of showing activities (tasks or events) displayed against time. On the left of the chart is a list of the activities and along the top is a suitable time scale. Each activity is represented by a bar; the position and length of the bar reflects the start date, duration and end date of the activity. This allows you to see at a glance:

- What the various activities are

- When each activity begins and ends

- How long each activity is scheduled to last

- Where activities overlap with other activities, and by how much

- The start and end date of the whole project.

To summarise, a Gantt chart shows you what has to be done (the activities) and when (the schedule).

Task Name	Q1 2009			Q2 2009			Q3 2009	
	Dec '08	Jan '09	Feb '09	Mar '09	Apr '09	May '09	Jun '09	Jul '09	Aug
Planning		▨▨▨▨							
Research			▨▨▨▨						
Design				▨▨▨					
Implementation					▨▨▨▨▨▨				
Follow up								▨▨	

A simple Gantt chart

Gantt Chart History

The first Gantt chart was devised in the mid 1890s by Karol Adamiecki, a Polish engineer who ran a steelworks in southern Poland and had become interested in management ideas and techniques. Some 15 years after Adamiecki, Henry Gantt, an American engineer and management consultant, devised his own version of the chart and it was this that became widely known and popular in western countries. Consequently it was Henry Gantt whose name was to become associated with charts of this type.

SOURCE: www.gantt.com

You might try the Coin Tossing Test

Take two ideas. Assign one to Heads and one to Tails. The toss of a coin is going to decide which one takes priority. Toss the coin. It's Heads. You either say "yippee" in your heart in which case your gut and the coin are in accord. Or you are saying "darned" in which case the Tail project takes priority. Or you are just not quite sure – in which case offer yourself the best of 3 tosses…but don't do any more because you need to make a decision, and your simple act of not-sureness is the decision. Tail project takes priority.

All your work with Time, Talent and Treasure may have shown a real opportunity to move one idea forward more quickly than another. Great. Go for it.

"Everyone who has taken a shower has had an idea. It's the person who gets out of the shower, dries off, and does something about it that makes a difference"

Nolan Bushell, Founder of Atari. Quoted in *How to Have Kick-Ass Ideas*

Whatever happens now, you need to make a plan. Start somewhere and get going.

The Soldier: ill at ease

The next reason people visit a CGO surgery in their Soldier years is because they feel uncomfortable with where they are in the world. Maybe they have been working on the fringes of success for too long, and see their colleagues reaching greatness, wealth, acclaim.

In this case we try and explore their skill base and see how rich a character they are already. Some people build incredibly deep roots. That takes a long time to establish, and then, when they have their great idea / great opportunity they are later in life but more experienced than many. They are richer in skills and more able to withstand the pressures on them.

Others rise straight to the sun, get an amazing break early in life, and then find it difficult to repeat the success or stay at the top.

Not everyone is going to win an Oscar, run the Tate, direct a mega hit, or write a bestseller but we can all make a difference using our creativity. It can be self-destructive to wish for "what might have beens" or think in terms of "if only."

We all have moments, and part of the role of the Soldier is to fight those self-doubts by taking time, and maybe seek skilled support.

There is an amazing worksheet created by Byron Katie, who is an American who found the strength to pull herself out of the gutter and now writes and lectures around the world. It is available free to download.

The key mantra of her programme is to consider "Where would you be without that thought?" If you didn't feel that the world owed you a living, or that you hated x for getting the job you wanted, or you wished you'd chosen a different path at some point, where would you be? How would you feel? Perhaps more free, lighter in your mood, and more able to consider the way forward from where you are now?

I would suggest you download The Work, as she calls it, and if you have something to tackle – go to work. www.thework.com

At New Year we often write down Resolutions. Here are a series of questions which can be tried at any time. [I'm sorry I can't spot the source of them.]

Aspirations and Intentions

Review the last 12 months
(Find something good that happened to you each month)

Where do you want to go from here, now?

What adventure/s is/are calling you?

What would make your heart sing?

Who do you want to meet?

What is/are your word/s for the year?

What will your theme for this year be?

Then make a To Do list ...or rather two lists.

Me (to do, in my control)	Universe (to do for me please!)

Share your answers with a partner/friend and see how you can expand and grow the answers.

Coaching – A way through some mud

Although about half way through this book, this is the last section I wrote. Colleagues reading through felt there was a missing element to help Soldiers and Judges and those still mewling at mid-career. For me, Coaching and being Coached has been a fantastic missing link, now forged.

After 30 years of "just doing it", I decided it would be good to take a moment of reflection. I'd heard about Coaching and was delighted to find that Rachael Stevens, who I had known through Old Vic New Voices, was training with the Coaching Academy www.the-coaching-academy.com to be a Personal Performance Coach. I have mentioned her and the process earlier in the Time section above. I thought it might be useful to look at some of the techniques which you might use yourself, or for which you may seek guidance.

I was looking at whether to go freelance again, after 3 years with a safe pay cheque coming in. Rachael introduced me to the GROW model which invites you to explore the following:

G = Your Goal – what are you striving to achieve and what will it look like when you get there? This might be a short-term Goal or a long-term quite aspirational Goal. The coaching process allows us to talk around it and gently reach a SMART one – using the business acronym of Specific, Measurable, Attainable, Realistic, Timely.

In my case, I wanted to see whether I could focus my fee/earning time into 3 days a week of contracts, allowing me a day to service this work, and 3 more days for my own personal development and to offer my surgeries. I set a date by which I wanted this Goal to be in place (Timely). I worked out how much I needed to earn over a year, and what that would mean on a daily fee basis to achieve that target (Measurable). We then looked at it and explored whether it was Realistic. Would people out there actually pay me that daily fee? Then we looked at whether it was Attainable. Was there a market out there? Could I reach a target client base (narrowcast marketing) and was there competition that might knock me off kilter?

I explored how reaching the Goal will make me feel. What

it will sound like. What it will look like. How I will describe myself when I have achieved my Goal.

And at this point we looked at Regrets. What might an 80 year old me look back on and recommend to the 56 year old me as I am today? What might I regret at 80 if I had not gone for the Goal? How might my life look different and feel different in 3 years time if I do nothing, or if I go for the Goal?

R = Your Reality – where am I now. What's the reality of my situation? If my Goal is to run a 4 minute mile (which it isn't) then do I currently get out of breath running to the bus?

This is the point when a Coach can help you look at yourself rather more deeply. They begin to introduce the concept of Limiting Beliefs. To re-quote the Henry Ford aphorism, "If you think you can or you think you can't you're probably right." But anything (or nearly anything) is possible if you believe in yourself. If you always believe you forget names, you probably do. If you make a conscious effort to remember names, and believe that you can – it's amazing what you can achieve.

Over a number of weeks, Rachael and I explored my Reality and my Limiting Beliefs. There are many different models which people use, and different acronyms, but at their heart they seem to me to be much the same.

I was recently introduced to the Traffic Light drama game and wonder whether this might be useful to Reality and from there onward to Options. Red – what would I like to stop doing? Amber – what would I like to be ready to do? Green – what would I like to continue doing?

O = Your Options – looking at the many, or few, ways to work towards the Goal. Finding a niche for your skills and interests seems key to much of this. And then letting your mind run free.

Nothing should be off-limits at this point. You are looking

at all the ways in which you might attain your Goal. Maybe keep it legal and decent, honest and true – but otherwise go wild! Spot when you are limiting yourself. Just make a note of an Option where you say, "I'd love to but I can't/won't/couldn't/shouldn't because…"

What if money were no object? What if space were no object? What if responsibilities were no object? What if time were no object? Just look at a list of options and then see what is holding you back from choosing it.

Part of the role of a Coach is to question you around all this area. Slowly helping you reach a series of Options that make sense for you: moving from your current Reality towards a Goal.

Remember that Coaching is not Therapy. Nor is it counseling or consultancy. These are different skills and different mindsets. Being careful not to stray into giving advice (consultancy) or exploring personal issues looking backwards into the client's past (therapy) is very important. In Coaching, you are looking at the present reality and the way ahead to a Goal.

W = Your Will Do list – This is the action list. What I do to get there. When it needs to be done. What I need to clear from my reality so I can start on the future. With whom do I need to share my Goal to improve my chances?

Again, whether the Goal is short or long, make the action points SMART. Write them down. And then check in to see how you are doing along the way.

Did I reach my Goal? Yes. With the help of Rachael, and the willpower that I gained through the Coaching process I have, for two years now, hit my target. It has allowed me to take time to do more CGO Surgeries. It has allowed me to take time to write this book. And it is allowing me to train as a Coach.

Another tool worth exploring is the Wheel of Life. Again widely available on the web but it truly benefits to work with an experienced Coach to see how best to explore its power.

A quick google will show you many examples. In essence you take a circle and subdivide it into, say, 8 segments. Each segment represents a priority in your life. You choose the title for each segment – maybe money, family, church, art, holidays… whatever is one of your 8 priorities. Then colour each segment out from the centre as far as you feel you are currently satisfied with where you are. Most wheels split the segments into 10 marks out to the edge. If you colour up to mark 6 you are 60% satisfied with where you are at the moment. (Image source www.miruscoaching.org/Wheel_of_Life.html)

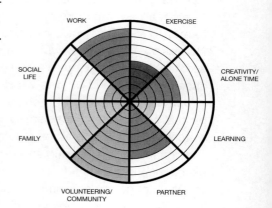

Then you wonder with your Coach what it would mean to be at 10 on one or more of these segments – and what could you do now to move just one step closer. If exercise satisfaction is currently at 5 or 50% of completely satisfied, what could you do to get to 60% satisfied.

The Coaching Academy has a great 2-day, completely free introduction to all of this. I am sure there are many other similar free or paid programmes. There are loads on the web. And then come and find a suitable coach.

There are so many tools which come through the Coaching world. So many models and acronyms, helpful books and courses. I recommend thinking about the process and seeing whether you could benefit from some Coaching at this stage of life. Or indeed whether you might enjoy re-training as a Coach.

Necessary Theatre

As I pass through my Soldier years and head rapidly to Judge, I have realised that there is one thing that is most important to me. To see, be involved in, and support something I call "Necessary Theatre", by which I mean theatre that I have to see; that I hope is going to move me deeply, or show me an aspect of our world or lives which I had not thought about. In some way I hope to be changed, even be transformed, by the experience. Escapism is great, but I can get that watching a quick movie or reading an unnecessary book. The chance to be in an audience sharing a powerful creative experience is wonderful.

"Why not go out on a limb? That's where the fruit is", said Mark Twain. I love working with the next generation and supporting the creation of projects that work on that edge between consciousness and art, humanity and theatre.

It has taken me a while not to worry about the fact that my peers are running the RSC, or retiring as millionaires from their accounting practices, or celebrating the 10th anniversary of their West End shows. We were all Mewling and Puking together many years ago. Their paths have been rocky and tough, but rather single-minded. Mine has taken me all over the place – but I am now, with a decaf coffee or a nice cup of tea, helping the next generation to make "Necessary Theatre."

Hierarchy of Need

We in the creative arts have an immensely valuable part to play in serving the higher needs of humans, and commenting on the essential expectations of humans (especially where it is denied through famine, war, global warming, and the other joys of the human race).

If you are not familiar with Maslow's Hierarchy, here is a quick summary drawn from available sources on the web.

Maslow's Hierarchy

In 1943 Abraham Maslow, one of the founding fathers of humanist approaches to management, wrote an influential paper that set out five fundamental human needs and their hierarchical nature. They are quoted and taught so widely now that many people perceive this model as the definitive set of needs and do not look further.

The hierarchical effect

A key aspect of the model is the hierarchical nature of the needs. The lower the needs in the hierarchy, the more fundamental they are and the more a person will tend to abandon the higher needs in order to pay attention to sufficiently meeting the lower needs. For example, when we are ill, we care little for what others think about us: all we want is to get better.

Maslow called the first four needs "D-need" as they are triggered when we have a deficit. Only self-actualization is a need that we seek for solely positive reasons. Maslow also called them "instinctoid" as they are genetically programmed into us as essential for evolutionary survival. Loss of these during childhood can lead to trauma and lifelong fixation.

Note that in practice this hierarchy is only approximate and you do not have to have your physiological needs fully satisfied before going on to seeking higher needs. In their global survey, for example, Tay and Diener (2011) found that people can be living in hazardous poverty and yet still derive much satisfaction from having social needs (belonging and esteem) fulfilled.

The five needs

- **Physiological needs** are to do with the maintenance of the human body. If we are unwell, then little else matters until we recover.

- **Safety needs** are about putting a roof over our heads and keeping us from harm. If we are rich, strong and powerful, or have good friends, we can make ourselves safe.

- **Belonging needs** introduce our tribal nature. If we are helpful and kind to others they will want us as friends.

- **Esteem needs** are for a higher position within a group. If people respect us, we have greater power.

- **Self-actualization needs** are to "become what we are capable of becoming", which would be our greatest achievement.

Three more needs

These are the needs that are most commonly discussed and used. In fact Maslow later added three more needs by splitting two of the above five needs.

Between esteem and self-actualization needs was added:

- Need to know and **understand**, which explains the cognitive need of the academic.

- The need for **aesthetic beauty**, which is the emotional need of the artist.

Self-actualization was divided into:

- Self-actualization, which is realizing one's own potential, as above.

- Transcendence, which is helping others to achieve their potential.

So what?

Using it

To distract people from higher needs, threaten their lower needs. It is no surprise that poison has been effectively used to bring down kings and princes without necessarily killing them.

Perceive and help people to meet the needs on which they currently focused. Their attention is here and they will thank you for assistance in meeting their present needs.

Encourage them to reach up to higher needs. Let them see and reach up to the greater things in life. Create a tension which you can use for your purpose.

Defending

Seek only needs at your current level. Neither retreat too rapidly to lower needs nor reach too quickly for higher needs. When you are ready, only then reach in your own time for higher needs. If other people seek to help you, you may accept their help but are not obliged to repay in any way their demand.

See also

CIN Model, Argyris' Model 1, Murray's Needs, Evolution

References

Maslow (1943), Maslow and Lowery (1998)

Tay L, and Diener E. (2011). Needs and subjective well-being around the world. Journal of Personal Social Psychology, 101, 2, 354-65.

Source: www. changingminds.org
Welcome to ChangingMinds.org, the largest site in the world on all aspects of how we change what others think, believe, feel and do. There are already around 5500 pages here, all free and with much more to come.

So – as a Soldier you are gaining Wisdom. You are where you are. Spending time wishing you were somewhere else is a waste of energy. You have connections. You have begun to understand what it is to be human in a way that may be forgotten, or unknown, in earlier years.

Maybe you are concerned about the Planet. Maybe you have dependents. Maybe you are aware of your position across the Maslow levels. Maybe you are aware of "Here" as you "Take A Moment to Reflect", again, on David Wagoner's poem:

"Stand still. The trees ahead and the bushes beside you
are not lost.
Wherever you are is called Here,
And you must treat it as a powerful stranger,
Must ask permission to know it and be known.
The forest breathes. Listen. It answers,
I have made this place around you,
If you leave it, you may come back again, saying Here.
No two trees are the same to Raven.
No two branches are the same to Wren.
If what a tree or a branch does is lost on you
Then you are surely lost.
Stand still. The forest knows where you are.
You must let it find you."

David Wagoner – Lost

A Spiritual Conspiracy

On the surface of the world right now there is war and violence and things seem dark. But calmly and quietly, at the same time, something else is happening underground.
An inner revolution taking place and certain individuals are being called to a higher Light.

It is a silent revolution
From the inside out.
From the ground up.
This is a global operation.
A Spiritual Conspiracy.
There are sleeper cells in every nation on the planet.
You won't see us on the TV
You won't read about us in the newspaper
You won't hear about us on the radio
We don't seek any glory

We don't wear any uniform
We come in all shapes and sizes, colours and styles
Most of us work anonymously
We are quietly working behind the scenes
In every country and culture of the world
Cities big and small,
mountains and valleys,
In farms and villages, tribes and remote islands
You could pass by one of us on the street and not even notice →

Justice – and Wise Saws

When you've been around the block a few times, when you have a position of responsibility, then we all sometimes believe we know best. We are a little wiser than we were at the start, but we are also older and potentially out of touch. They say that you are born in your own era and can't change. I may work with the Millennium Generation and be teaching Generation Y and soon Z, but I am born and think as a Baby Boomer. There's lots more about Generations on www.socialmarketing.org/newsletter/features/generation1.htm

My proposition is that our desires to work in the Creative industries, and the basic principles of developing opportunities, learning our craft, supporting others, team work and delivering projects have not changed. Marketing has not changed. Some of the tools have got shinier and faster. The web has offered us phenomenal free opportunities to stretch our budgets.

Some things, however, have changed, and we as Wise Saws need to understand this.

Our potential audience is overwhelmed with opportunities to spend their limited time, and even more limited treasure on leisure. So our persuasive message has to attract people to the experience we offer, and be incredibly carefully targeted.

Our planet is being destroyed by the human race. The attention that we place on leisure is tempered by the attention we must surely place on protecting Mother Earth for future generations. The arts can offer a window into this challenge, and awaken consciousness which is numbed by so much of the tabloid press.

There is a growing movement for speaking from our core and connecting our humanity through heart connections. Much of our potential audience understands more about the power of love, health, and spiritual balance than was considered (or at least voiced) by previous generations. For me the arts and creative practice can offer so much human healing and support to humanity in this area. What I have earlier termed "Necessary Theatre."

And on the counter side, there is a cynicism about the arts and creative industries among so many of the powers that could make such a difference to the quantity and quality of arts provision in this country and the world. A Swedish politician was

→

We go undercover
We remain behind the scenes.
It is of no concern to us
Who takes the final credit
But simply that the work gets done.
Occasionally we spot each other in the street
We give a quiet nod and continue on our way
During the day, many of us pretend we have normal jobs

But behind the false storefront at night
Is where the real work takes place
Some call us the Conscious Army
We are slowly creating a new world
With the power of our minds and hearts
We follow, with passion and joy.

Our orders come to us from Central Spiritual Intelligence
We are dropping soft, secret love bombs when no-one is looking
Poems, hugs, music, photography, movies, kind words, smiles,
Meditation and prayer, dance, social activism, websites, blogs,
Random acts of kindness...

We each express ourselves in our own unique ways
With our own unique gifts and talents. →

→

'Be the change you want to see in the world.'
That is the motto that fills our hearts.
We know it is the only way real transformation takes place
We know that quietly and humbly we have the power of all the oceans combined.

Our work is slow and meticulous
Like the formation of mountains
It is not even visible at first glance
And yet with it, entire tectonic plates
Shall be moved in the centuries to come.
Love is the new religion of the 21st Century.
You don't have to be a highly educated person
Or have any exceptional knowledge to understand it
It comes from the intelligence of the heart
embedded in the timeless, evolutionary pulse of all human beings.

Be the change you want to see in the world.
Nobody else can do it for you
We are now recruiting.
Perhaps you will join us
Or already have.
All are welcome
The door is open.

Author unknown
Sent to me by email 120323

asked in 2008 at the time of the last crash how he would square his budget – what was he going to cut, the arts or hospitals. He answered **If I cut the arts I will have to build more hospitals**. [I heard this on the Today programme on Radio 4 but have not been able to trace the proper credit].

This Swedish politician got it. Whilst here, the arts suffer from a continuing thousand cuts. The good things that the arts can do to improve health and wellbeing, connect communities and disparate groups, to awaken the spirits of the very elderly and open the hearts of the very young are being put in danger. Short-term political decisions made to win the immediate favour of voters, protect the industries and powerhouses that keep politicians in socks, ignore the long-term effect of tiny cut, after cut, after cut, because that will be the next lot's problem.

So that, for me, is where we as Wise Saws find ourselves. We have Shining Morning Faces looking to be supported and inspired. We have to avoid the trap of looking back to a gentler time, of being angry and cynical. We have to be true to our hearts and offer coffee and chamomile tea to those who can carry the torch forward.

BLOG 130228

Chance encounters – and getting to "yes"...

I love it when I end up in an unexpected place, with unexpected people, and the universe offers me something to help me in the future. It happens so often to me that I wonder whether I am either very lucky, or I am practicing what I preach which is, in open space terms, *"be prepared to be surprised."*

On Sunday I was due to have a lovely relaxing afternoon and evening with my wife, Kath. I'd got it all planned. And then out of the blue, she receives an invitation to read an unknown play, to support an emerging director get their head around a text before pitching for funding. So I had two options...have a lovely relaxing evening alone, or get my stuff together and head over to a flat in Dalston and listen to some play thing.

"If you think you can or you think you can't you're probably right..."

Henry Ford

Well, you've guessed it, I did the thing. We arrived for a delicious dinner in a tiny apartment in Dalston, the home of actor Loren O'Dair with whom I'd worked on *Dick Turpin*, where she delighted us with her Black Bess. After dinner with the 5 actors, the scripts were distributed and a rather surreal and unexpected play unfolded.

There's something special about being in a tiny flat and being asked to consider a play which may end up in full production. This wasn't a new work, but rather the re-exploration of a piece that had been high profile in a major producing house in the 90s. Why did it work then? Could it work today? Is it reliant on stars to carry it? Will the voices around this dinner table do it justice for the director? Fascinating way to see theatre.

Chance encounter 1: one of the actors was at RADA with my son, seemed perfect for speaking classic dense text, and I was able to recommend her to a senior director colleague working on restoring the repertoire of plays from the Georgian period. Hope they end up working together.

What are you thinking?

Then for two days this week I went to an inspiring course in Birmingham for myself – a chance to review how I live and work. How I relate to others and understand myself. And how to set goals for myself to realise what I want. "If you think you can or you think you can't you're probably right..." Henry Ford. I pay tribute to Richard Jackson, the inspired creator of the Winning Edge programme www.mancroftinternational.com. I have never written so many notes, thought so hard about myself, or reached so many very simple realisations. Thank you Richard.

Chance encounter 2: one of my co-students works at a senior level in a major telecoms company and when I shared my vision for a project called StoryMusic2020, enabling 197 nations to talk to each other, and compose/create together, he knew just the man to approach to get some advice and possible involvement.

So, for me, the last few days have been about taking chance encounters and making them work. I've just come off Skype with a director based in Latvia and London exploring how to raise money for her new show – and whilst we were talking I thought I'd google ideas for the show and try to find companies in Riga who might have a few bob to spare. First random word search generated a major international company based in the city, doing exactly the technological design idea she needs to make her show extra-ordinary. I hope they are as excited by her vision, as I was in finding this design company.

Wise Saws – As we get older we may have learned to be fearful of failure, but if you have kept your inner child then you can still play, experiment, and search for the unexpected. If you are "Prepared to Be Surprised", then you bring your wisdom to support your child. You know where to look to find juicy new ideas and helpful information. Use that wisdom.

We are all critics now

It is so easy to express our opinions without thinking, or to seek to impress with our knowledge. The arts and creative industries can sometimes be a bitchy place, where a laugh is gained by a quick gibe. These are human traits of which we all need to be wary. Earlier, we explored Patsy Rodenberg's "Circles of Energy" and the flow between the giver and the receiver, actor and audience, critic and reader. We need to listen to how our words will be heard, and where they will be heard, and the effect that they can have.

Having said all that, one man's bad review is another man's chip paper. But bad reviews can still hurt.

Kath was performing her one woman show "The Mother's Bones" at Edinburgh a few years ago. It was a deeply personal exploration of three generations of woman – mother, grandmother and daughter using the Persephone myth as a basis for her exploration. She played all three women using a personally created language style for each generation. There were no English language words, but the meaning of every moment was clear once we, the audience, had settled into the pace and sound of the piece. It was powerful and deeply moving for many of the audience.

We awoke one morning and she rushed out to get *The Scotsman,* because we thought there would be a review. There was. It was a brief and dismissive 2 star review: the writer just didn't get the show. Kath was devastated. It hit her hard and very personally. She literally crawled under the duvet and cried. So much personal passion and care had been put into conceiving this show, reflecting her relationship with her own mother as she celebrated her 80th birthday, and the children and grandchildren who were part of her matriarchal clan.

Devastating. I wasn't sure what to do next. I wasn't sure she would be able to perform later that morning. The last thing she needed was a phone call from a mate, presumably commiserating.

But the phone call was from a friend in Edinburgh and it wasn't to commiserate. It was to cheer Kath's 5 star lead review in that day's *Metro*, seen by hundreds of people as they travelled on Edinburgh's buses and trains that morning.

As you can imagine, the dark clouds parted, the sun shone through, and less than 10 minutes after she was under the duvet, Kath couldn't wait to get to the theatre and inspire another audience with her piece.

We are all human. I find it hard to fully believe the actors who say they never read, hear about, or sense the nature of their critical reviews. If they don't – good for them, but I think I'd like to hear the cheers, and ride with the clouds.

However, in this age of the Internet everyone can be a critic, and it seems many of them are writing without being in a place of wisdom and considered practice. So my charge to myself, and all those Justices who are asked (or choose) to comment on shows is to do so from a place of understanding, knowledge, and Second Circle.

BLOG 120620

We are all critics now – but some are more objective / professional

I've just picked up a coffee from a theatre foyer and overheard two of the staff discussing a show they'd seen in their group last night. "A bit rubbish" was the verdict. Fortunately, I'd already seen it, and it most definitely wasn't rubbish (in my opinion) – and featured one performance which will stay with me for many months. Word of mouth still remains the most powerful form of good publicity, and overheard critical conversations can be dangerous for an organisation too. I guess the lesson I take away, as someone responsible for the communications and impressions given by a theatre and its programme to the outside world at Bury St Edmunds, is make sure this example is told to all our volunteers and staff who work front-of-house. Strongly voiced negative opinions are not good for business.

As Udderbelly runs on the Southbank, and the Edinburgh Festival prepares to set sail, and as festivals all over Britain happen where there is too much choice,

> Space for thoughts

and we have too little time to see everything, remember word of mouth in the marketing mix.

But remember that we have some of the most respected, experienced and dedicated reviewers anywhere in the world seeing literally hundreds of shows in a year. Some have 20-30 years experience of seeing theatre, or dance, or opera. They have a way with words to excite audiences, or to dash hype and overblown expectation. So as well as listening to the two staff behind the coffee counter, and the comments from people in the fringe ticket queue, make sure you read the critical opinions of at least 2 or 3 of the newspaper journalists or bloggers who most, appear, to share your views. Be swayed by them...but then take a risk and don't always believe them. [One story – I was house manager of Bristol Hippodrome when the Old Vic Company brought the Scottish play with Peter O'Toole in the title role, and Brian Blessed famously doused in a bucket of blood as a very larger than life ghost. The reviews nationally were so so so awful, and the surrounding press so bad, that everyone in Bristol knew about the show weeks before it arrived in town. And they booked in their thousands because they couldn't believe it was as bad as the critics said. It was packed, and I stood each night as an audience went in expectant of something special/unusual/extraordinary, and then I stood as they walked out silent/stunned/bemused... with one shared comment...the critics were right, we should have believed them.]

Happy theatregoing – and don't listen too attentively to two young students behind a coffee counter telling each other that last night was "rubbish."

BLOG 131022

Online ranting for self-aggrandisement

I've been silent for a few weeks, for personal reasons, not because of a loss of love with the theatre or the people it is my pleasure to work with. Mother's funeral tomorrow, house nearly sold, executor role nearly sorted, and the end of 7 years of getting to know more about Alzheimer's than I wanted to. By the way, can I recommend *Contented Dementia* by Oliver James as a most helpful book for anyone supporting a loved one with Alzheimer's or supporting a colleague who is trying to work out how best to deal with someone with this horrid disease. It talks of red and green memories, and understanding that is the key to helping.

I am driven to write to vent a little bit of anger. I'm on Facebook and enjoy a daily look at who's saying what, and the occasional longer trawl through. It's a very public medium and I learn a lot – sometimes I learn more than I want.

Today I come across a series of rants and raves following one person's visit to see a new show in preview. He's wondering how to tell someone involved in the show that he didn't enjoy it. His medium of expression is to broadcast his dislike to his 575 Facebook friends. Some of them in turn respond with their own vitriol or unhappy feelings – and this message broadcasts further outwards to their own hundreds and thousands of friends.

Now we are all "members of the public" and can all have opinions which we wish to vent – but most of his, and most of my, friends are in the business and I believe

"A critic is a man who knows the way, but cannot drive the car." Kenneth Tynan

we have a responsibility to support any creative team and company as they move through rehearsals, previews, re-writes and changes to get to the press night. Even then, I think we have a duty to be very careful how our criticism is delivered because, like the official press critics, people do take notice of what we say.

If I rant off about seeing a show I don't like on Facebook, or here through this Blog, it is going to be read by other friends and colleagues who know me and know I blow hot and cold about shows. It is also going to be read by potential ticket buyers who might think twice. And most important the carefully written phrases of damnation or faint praise will be read by those involved with the show. It cannot do them any good, to have my stuff heaped on their shoulders, whether they agree or not.

"And the end of all our exploring
Will be to arrive where we started
And know the place for the first time."

TS Eliot

So I started this morning cross, and wanted to share with the Reader.

I am often asked to see new work at first reading, or in a showcase evening. This work is fragile and in need of care and attention. It is sometimes not easy to give supportive criticism. There will be some work that I just don't like. It is still a pleasure to try and help the writers and those involved see the next steps for their writing. It is great to do this with another observer, so we complement each other in our comments and thoughts. Some of those on Facebook that I read this morning should clearly be kept away from this process.

To quote Thumper in Bambi, and the fantastic quest secretary, Jean-Marie Feddercke, from Buxton and Oxford QuestFest: " If you can't say something nice, don't say nuthin' at all". Unless of course you are engaged as a public critic, attending after press night, and ready to share your personal opinion with your public.

Remember the 3 blocks rule

In New York it is talked about because the city is made up of blocks on a grid system. As you come out of the theatre you gather outside and you have no idea who you are rubbing shoulders with. It may be an investor, the leading actor's mother, the producer, or the casting director you have always wanted to meet, but you don't recognise their face.

If you proceed to talk in a loud stage whisper about how dreadful the show is you will not know who can hear. You may be hurting someone badly, you may be clocked by that casting director as trouble, or you may just be making a fool of yourself because of your opinionated rant.

So walk away, with your friends until you are 3 blocks away, and then, if you must, have your rant.

And remember next time you go to an audition or a meeting and someone you recognise, but can't quite put a name to, asks you what you thought of such and such a show or such and such a play, breathe and don't say the first rude thing that comes to mind. Because sure as eggs is eggs, that person you are about to talk to is the director, author, or casting director of said play.

A few thoughts?

So Thumper is right: "If you can't say something nice, don't say nuthin' at all." Sometimes you should express your views – but just be careful to whom you are speaking. You can never control your audience on Facebook. You should be very careful when meeting a stranger. So three pieces of advice: Know your audience. Three blocks rule. Don't say the first rude thing that comes to mind.

Conclusion – Inspired /Overwhelmed

Then, a **soldier**,
Full of strange oaths, and bearded like the pard,
Jealous in honor, sudden, and quick in quarrel,
Seeking **the bubble reputation**
Even in the cannon's mouth. And then the **justice**,
In fair round belly with good capon lined,
With eyes severe and beard of formal cut,
Full of **wise saws** and modern instances;
And so he plays his part.

Here are 10 points from this section for further reflection:

1. Take a moment to reflect

2. Isolate the time needed to pay the bills

3. Remember the folks who you know who have money!!

4. Network with business and non-arts fraternities

5. Gather talent to support you/kill unnecessary ones

6. We can change lives with our creativity

7. Know what would make your heart sing

8. Be the change that you want to see in the world

9. Be a careful and responsible critic

10. Begin to know yourself

Despairing / Stuck

Slippered Pantaloon –
the tired creative artist

One of the challenges of working in the creative industries is that some people make a fortune, the rest find it hard to make a living. The lucky ones have found some way to gather some savings, or are in a position where their outgoings are small enough to allow time to make creative work effectively. Most of us will need to work until we drop – and whilst buying a weekly Lottery ticket isn't going to guarantee a rosy future, it's nice to dream.

I have said for years that I would love to retire, by which I mean not have to get up and earn a living each day to pay the mortgage. I would get up with a spring in my step and help to make creative arts happen, just as I hope I do now – but without the nagging worry of the end of the month and the overdraft.

So this section is dedicated to those who have worked hard making creative projects happen, and have to find the strength and reserve to keep doing it.

Being surrounded by the energy of creative artists is, for me, a way of relieving my tiredness – and being able to offer some ideas of mistakes to avoid, or people to speak with is such a good way to keep me feeling there is a point to life. Open Space is one place where that always happens. Each year I make my annual pilgrimage to "D & D". As I type this, I am a week away from being at the 9th annual Devoted and Disgruntled event at York Hall, run by Improbable theatre company. I will meet scores of creative artists who are devoted to theatre and the wider arts, and disgruntled by the state of the world, or our place within it. We will debate using Open Space Technology, which is the most freeing form of structure for important debate to happen, where no moment of your time is wasted.

BLOG 120303

Whatever happens is the only thing that could have

This is one of the guiding principals of life, and of Open Space Technology (OST). This is a rather wonderful and extraordinary method of holding meetings, that gets the things discussed which you want to be discussed, that marginalises egos, that generates action plans, and at which you should prepare to be surprised. For seven years, Improbable have been using this methodology/philosophy to hold a gathering of creative artists who wish to tackle the key question, **"What are we doing about theatre and the performing arts?"** Not what are they going to do – what are we doing. And who is we? Well, simply, The Right People.

The gathering is open to everyone, and this weekend there were 300+ people gathered in York Hall, Bethnal Green in east London to tackle the question. We started with no agenda items, and a blank sheet of paper. After 2.5 days we had addressed around 120 issues chosen by the attendees. We walked away with a bound set of reportage of around 90 of those meetings. We were inspired, frustrated, moved, excited, tired, tearful, delighted, sorted, unsorted, befriended, loud, silent, chanting, singing, drawing and even beginning the process of making small sacred dolls imbued with our heart and love which, when 700 are created will represent the love that we can offer to the 7 billion people on our planet.

Whoever comes are the right people is one of the guiding principles. There's no point in wishing x or y or z was in the room, entering the discussion. But we can now, a few days after the event, think of the people we'd like to have in the room with us next year – and that most definitely includes you. One of the wonderful things about Devoted and Disgruntled is that 300+ people gather in a single circle at the start of the day without badges, without being introduced. Should you choose to be there anonymously, because you wish to speak from your heart and not represent the views of your own organisation, or because you want time to listen without judgement from others – then that is your right and privilege.

You are just the person we need to tackle one (or more) of the subjects that need debating. And maybe I'm just the person you need to help you with something you need.

It is hard to explain. It is impossible to summarise what happens. It is immensely carefully held by Phelim McDermott and his Improbable colleagues. And it is extraordinarily simple.

Did we solve the problems of the universe? Well, we solved a few things people needed solving, we tackled a few thorny subjects that needed airing, we had a few quick wins, and we have work to do. **When it's over, it's over** is another principle; for some items on the agenda, it is over and sorted. For others, the space will open again at another time, for still more work to be done by us to make our world of the theatre and the performing arts a better place.

Personally, I have to say this is an annual fix...a way to kick-start a creative year. It is a bit daunting the first hour or so, but don't be put off. We really want you there with us next year. You are just the person we need to tackle one (or more) of the subjects that need debating. And maybe I'm just the person you need to help you with something you need. Let's meet at York Hall early 2013 and see...over a cup of tea and an egg or bacon butty.

Open Space Technology

Anyone can plan and run an Open Space event. You can download the tools for free from the web Here's one site http://www.openspaceworld.com/users_guide.htm. You can attend D&D and watch a master. And then you can/could offer your services to a new sector of the world where Open Space is less well known as a tool.

I have been lucky enough to be engaged half a dozen times to help shape a debate in the medical profession around Patient care, and the priorities to be adopted by regional Clinical Commissioning Groups (GP surgeries working together). I don't need to know the areas they want to debate. I need to be able to hold the space and facilitate the meeting in a calm and supportive way. I need to trust OST to work. I have not been let down yet, and I have been invited back to work again with the same people.

Here is my promotional sheet, introducing the principles of Open Space. Delighted to talk more about it with anyone who wants to use the tools. I have used it in my Anglia Ruskin teaching and in networking events. It works. As you read the next promotional pages, just wonder whether it could inspire you to do something differently, or allow you to be inspired differently.

How to make a meeting really count
We invite you to talk to us if the outcome matters to you

Open Space Technology is a process for running a conference or meeting, created 20 years ago by Harrison Owen. It has been used throughout the world in everything from the peace process to creating Broadway musicals. It offers any business or communicating organisation three key advantages for its staff/delegates at a meeting:

- Impact through freedom
- Inspiration through structure
- Involvement through engagement.

In addition to that, it is easy to plan and far cheaper than flying in key-note speakers; or trying to conceive the perfect break-out session. Let Open Space determine the structure, and then set the delegates to work. And prepare to be surprised.

Open Space is there to get "business" done and having a real business issue which needs work is the key. Harrison Owen suggests the issue should have **Complexity** (can't be solved by two people in a room), **Diversity** (where a range of people could have input and opinions), **Passion**, **Conflict** (maybe passions run high, maybe there are conflicting pressures) and **Urgency** (it needs to be solved yesterday).

The role of the facilitator is to establish the framework in which the creativity of the participants can be best harnessed; to explain the structure and the system; to prepare the atmosphere for Open Space to work; to get out of the way and let it happen; and believe in one of the core principals – *"Whatever happens is the only thing that could have."*

Whether it's an open invitation to a community of staff, audience and volunteers to engage in the future of their

theatre, or a gathering of 250 doctors and patients charged with setting the agenda for a Patient Revolution in West Suffolk, the process is the same. The participants are the passionate ones, and often the most knowledgeable about their chosen subject. The challenge is to take 250 people sitting in a circle (or horseshoe above) and get every one of them talking about what they need to engage in to feel their voice has been heard.

Impact through freedom

Starting with a provocative title offering the need for debate, action and involvement, we offer the delegates a blank agenda, and a time-space matrix which needs filling. There are slots of time in various spaces where issues can be discussed. This freedom to set the agenda, and raise any and every topic important to one or more people in the room is what offers participants the maximum opportunity for involvement. Add to this a few principles and one law…*"the law of two feet"*…and each person can use their time to be most impactful.

The law of two feet (or law of mobility) is an empowering device we could all benefit from using more often. When we are in a gathering and we are not being useful; or we have made our contribution and others are now getting on with the discussion; or we know we could make a difference by being in a different place – then use the law of two feet. Get up and politely move on. Go and use your skills where they are most needed. How about that as a suggestion when you are next in a meeting which was set to start on the hour, for an hour, and you know, sure as anything, that everyone will keep talking for an hour – before moving to another meeting somewhere else, on the hour, for an hour.

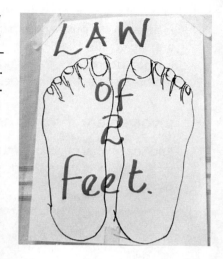

Introduce the law of two feet into your work. It could save hours.

Inspiration through structure

The process of facilitating Open Space is essentially one of atmosphere and preparation, and then careful introduction to the process and framework. As people begin to realise that their voice can be heard, that their subject will be discussed,

and that they can have an impact then many people become inspired. Very quickly the participants take the microphone and voice their individual provocation (see left), and the agenda board fills up (see right) with many sessions across the broadest spectrum of debate.

Involvement through engagement

And finally what could be better than the sight of every person in the room engaged and involved in a truly democratic process?

Finding New Inspiration

After an Open Space event, be it D&D or one you have run yourself, hopefully you will have new ideas, new contacts, and a bit of a new spark.

If not, then I suggest you look in the most extraordinary and unexpected directions. I'm looking out across Mounts Bay in Cornwall as I write this, in a tiny cottage that gives me a sense of space, and sky, and rain and wind. Last Christmas, I joined family in Byron Bay Australia for a big celebration with the Matriarchal clan gathered from the USA, London, Sydney, Essex and Suffolk. Here's what inspired me...

BLOG 130106

Returning from Australia

I've just had the pleasure of spending 3 weeks with family in Sydney and Byron Bay. I have to admit to not seeing a single moment of legit theatre. However, I was surrounded by the extraordinary theatre of that amazing country, and experienced being there at the end of the Mayan calendar for the Uplift Festival in Byron. Those who know me will be well aware that I have been intrigued since schooldays by the mystery of the unknown – I even used to put it on my cv to give "reading and theatre" a bit more bite, when I had little track record of career and life.

I witnessed the most amazing experiential theatre and it has left me with a sense of a "big idea" which I am mulling over, since I have one more week working from home before the freelance contracts kick in for a new season. I almost have a plan, and it feels an exciting complement to my current work programme, and a perfect merging of many strands of my life – but that's for another blog in a few blogs time.

For the meantime I just want to share impressions that hit me so powerfully over this time, and in that place. I was lucky enough to be one of 300-400 who saw the dawn rise on 22nd Dec 2012 over the coast at Byron Bay beach in company with Aboriginal leaders; 2 members of the International Council of 13 indigenous grandmothers www.grandmotherscouncil.org; two young activists who form the Earth Guardians www.earthguardians.org who are so central to the discussion of the future care of our planet; a group of Tibetan monks who spend time in the Crystal Castle/ Byron community; a descendent of the Mayan people there for

Uplift, and many experts and visitors from all across the globe. The world is changing – maybe for the better – as the powerful groups of indigenous and energised people share their passion to challenge the rape of our planet in the name of short-term profit. I am fascinated to see how we as theatremakers can best contribute to the phenomenal work being undertaken by the heartfelt agitation of so many tribes across the planet.

Later the same morning, four of our family went to a ceremony by the Tibetan monks to help us focus on our hopes and fears for the future. Myself, three theatremakers from, variously Suffolk, Sydney and Boulder Colorado, and our 5 year-old niece – who is a richer fabricator of dreams and imagination than all of us put together – witnessed an age old ceremony from an age old monk in age old Nepalese, and it was joyful to be there.

So much theatre in one day – and we most definitely bemused much of the rest of the family on our return to basecamp. We continued to have a wonderful exploration of tiny corners of the extraordinary land of Australia and I returned to Suffolk rejuvenated and inspired.

What inspired you as a child? What made you go "wow"? Maybe now, dressed in your Slippered Pantaloons, is a good time to see whether you can find out more about the art-form that got away, or the subject you loved and were stopped from studying. The web is easier today than the library and bound copies of the Encyclopedia Brittanica which we had as our global resource. Go hunting and enjoy! And maybe re-read the first paragraph on page 87 with a few questions to ask yourself.

Authentic Artist Workshop

If you are an actor without work – take a moment to paint. If you are a musician who is not working – why not create a solo show about your artistry. If you are a teacher who feels stuck in drama schools – why not take time out to explore what makes you an artist and a wo/man, and make it into a show. And if you are a poet – take time to dance.

What inspired you as a child? What made you go "wow"? Maybe now, dressed in your Slippered Pantaloons, is a good time to see whether you can find out more about the art-form that got away, or the subject you loved and were stopped from studying.

We are creative beings. You have spent a life nurturing your creative art-form, and maybe not exploring other art-forms. Now is a time to nourish yourself... maybe change the slippers to dancing shoes, or put on the stripy pantaloons rather than the grey ones.

In December 2007, my wife Kath created a 3 day workshop in which artists could explore their practice in a safe space. Six artists gather together for 3 days to share, to witness, to discover, to experiment, and to play, with only as much critical assessment as they would like from their peers. The workshop has since run over 30 times, with many participants returning.

They come for one of three things (or a mix). They are working on an idea and wish to explore it in a safely held space. They need to refresh their creativity after a busy period, especially where they may have done a long "for-the-money" job. Or they are masters in one art-form and they want to play in another. They may have almost forgotten the joy of drawing, or singing, or poetic form. Here they can explore and see how different creative forms can blend together.

I am sure there are many workshops of this type. I just know the light shining in the eyes of almost every member of the collective of artists who have worked with Kath through the Authentic Artist workshop programme.

> "You have some pretty amazing capabilities! As a human being you are naturally creative. And although our creative instincts tend to become suppressed, we have all the resources to change that around"
>
> Barez-Brown "Kick-Ass Ideas"

> What's an artform you want to play with?

Some go on to work with Kath's mentors, Paul Oertel and Nancy Spanier, in their week-long residential events entitled "The Discipline of Freedom."

Whatever needs shaking up, exploring, or a new sense of childlike "wow"ness – a workshop might be exactly the place to try.

Alongside these workshops there are classes to re-enliven your body, your soul, your spirit, your sexual energy. Five Rhythms, Jin Shin Jyutsu self-help, Yoga, Pilates, Tantra, Biodanza, Chi Kung, TaiChi, walking in nature, Singing, Gardening, Meditation, Pottery.

Something will work for you. Although, like me, you may have, in your Slippered Pantaloon phase, resistance to trying some of the new-fangled things being offered, take a chance.

Do you need Coffee or Chamomile Tea? Maybe you need a CGO Surgery. You will be most welcome.

One theme runs through much of this book. That is the need to listen. Listen to what you need, what your body needs, to stay creatively healthy and of course physically healthy. Listen to what your friends need. Listen to the changing world and see how your creativity can help that world. As we get into our Slippers we have more time to Listen…even if we may need to make copious notes for future reference.

BLOG 120818

Time to listen

It's so easy to be too busy to take the time to listen. To take the time to focus all your attention on someone else and see how you can help them to realise their dreams, or feel better about themselves. But if we can do it for someone else, then there's even more chance of people doing it for us when we need it.

There's an oft repeated remark from famous people that they achieved overnight success after years of work...look back in your theatre programmes and see who you saw on the way up. You may have worked with them as a stage manager or colleague actor. You may have seen them on the stage and cheered them. Stars do not achieve celestial glory overnight (usually) and for many it is too easy for the bright glimmer of stardom to be quashed by not being nurtured or cared for.

If you are in a position to listen, to help someone, to cheer someone to go further – then please do so, and you will be amazed at the return in the future.

I was asked to do a quick talk about the Theatre Royal for the Stowmarket Chamber of Commerce last week. A labour of love, since the meeting started at 6.45am (an unusual time for a bouncy talk about profit & loss and thespians). They did serve breakfast (even if I had to pay for my own). Sitting next to me was a very successful PR freelance who said she had come to the meeting especially to hear me. I was flattered, and even more so when I learned why. As a student she had contacted me when I ran Buxton Opera House to see whether I could give her any good advice about getting a job in marketing and PR in the arts. I met her, explored ideas, and suggested she contacted my successor at the Edinburgh International Festival to see if she could get a summer job. She did. He liked her. She joined the Festival. She stayed 2 years before moving on to the wider PR community. And now, 20+ years later she is in Suffolk, running her own highly successful business, Affinity PR, and sitting opposite me enjoying a plate of baked beans and fried egg too early in the morning.

I suppose, over 30 years, I've met hundreds of students like Helen. Today, in my CGO Surgeries, what I do that makes a difference is I listen. I give each person time. We seek to explore their life, their career, as if it was a first encounter with these particular problems for both of us. And by the way, you don't stop being needy of support and encouragement just because you've been in the biz 30 years. I got turned down for a part-time project with one of the major national theatre companies last month, having spent many hours honing my pitch and then visiting and meeting them. I went back to ask whether someone could spare a moment to call me and give me feedback. I've never done that before. I was encouraged to do that by talking to a young artist who had just been turned down, she'd rung for feedback, and had a brilliant, 45 minute, really helpful call from the organisation. She went away enriched, even if she didn't have the job. Sadly I wasn't so fortunate – I got a bland email from HR saying they had appointed someone who matched the criteria better. I of course wish that person good speed with a great project in a great organisation – but I'd have loved a bit of TLC and interest in "me". So as you see, it doesn't necessarily get any easier.

Next time someone asks for your advice, or a fraction of your time to share a dream, or some feedback – please think hard about what it could mean to them. You might help a star to shine brighter or just encourage someone to keep believing.

I continue to need to feed my own creative juices. I want to share ideas with senior players in the arts management and arts creativity sectors. I recently found a great outlet for that need, **MMM (Mission, Models and Money)** only to find after being at my first meeting that the funding had been cut and there would be no more amazing sessions in London that I could get to. Creative Scotland are funding MMM now and maybe I can make it up there to join back in with the discussions. The next Blog shares my joy in meeting fellow senior players and learning new things as a greybeard. Search out for other opportunities like this for yourself where there is time to listen and learn. Or make an opportunity for yourself and get away from the desk.

BLOG 120212

If we have little time left

If global economics are in free-fall, if world leaders appear paralysed to stop war and famine, if at home our communities are facing job losses and financial hardship, what can we do NOW, collectively or singly, to give hope, joy, relevance, and support to make the world a better place?

How do we reach out to those who do not naturally turn to our theatres and galleries, arts centres and orchestras, for spiritual and emotional support? How can we appear necessary and important to their lives? How do we raise our consiousness so we can do good together?

This is the series of questions I have pitched into the very early discussion stages of a new initiative of which I am really honoured to be a part. **MMM (Mission, Models and Money)** has been granted support for a programme called **re.volution** which brings together arts managers from across the UK, both virtually and in real rooms, to explore "building the resilience of creative practitioners and organisations and realising art and culture's leadership role in tackling the huge global challenges we face."

We've had one meeting, and the joy for me was that of the 12 practitioners gathered, I hadn't met a single one of them before. A completely new group of creative colleagues across the most diverse of creative sectors. I haven't got a clue how the next few months will shape up. What I do know is that I intend to try to find the time to be an active participant in discussion and meetings – just to see where it goes.

It is too easy for us as arts/creative practitioners to get bogged down in grant applications, staffing and volunteer support, contracting and making projects administratively sound, marketing the hell out of the tough sellers, raising every possible penny of fundraising to balance the books – and to forget that we are part of a glorious ecology of colleagues and friends who can make a difference.

Every day we have reasons to be grateful for the artistic/creative world we live in. Every day we can draw on the abundant gifts of the art-forms, the buildings and the colleagues with whom we work.

My question is, how do we use what we have wisely, at this time, to do the maximum good for humanity and the planet?

And don't get away with saying we can't change the world – who can ever tell which snowflake broke the branch?

I would welcome your thoughts by email chris@chrisgrady.org and I will feed them through into the MMM discussion also, with your permission.

Finally, in this section, when you are ready and can find the time to share your Talents, why not agree to join a Board of an arts organization?

If you have ever been an Arts Manager serving or reporting to a Board, you may feel that there is a level of frustration in the room. Are you preparing papers which no-one reads, seeking approval to projects that few around the table have considered carefully, and then answering questions from individuals which show their personal agendas and do not seem strategic or essential? It is often said that a building planning committee of a major arts organisation will take most time discussing the colour of the carpets, and least time understanding the contractual obligations being "let" on their behalf.

The only way to change a Board is to try and be a better Board Member from the inside. It comes back to the "know yourself" section (p79) when we looked at Belbin Types. Know your type. Know the types of your fellow Board members and then see how best you fit (or don't). If only some arts boards would use the Open Space principles for running meetings, then there would be a feeling of everything happening because it was necessary, and all of us offering our opinion in discussions where they are needed.

Here's a Blog which may be useful:

BLOG 111120

Why join a Board?

This weekend I've been on a Board retreat, working with 12 long-standing board members of one established organization. I then went off to assess whether I wanted to accept an invitation to join a fledgling board of a new theatre company. As a result, I spent 6 hours thinking about what makes a good board member, and then 2 hours trying to decide whether I liked a new group of people and could be a useful addition. I thought I'd share my thoughts, in case it's useful to existing Boards, those who serve/manage them, or to new companies.

We were wonderfully challenged by a facilitator at the first board retreat to enter a **thinking environment** and most importantly to bring attention to each other, be easy and open with each other (and honest), and to use the time to listen, speak thoughts, and address a key question: "What do I think makes a successful Board (and board member)?" Here is my list, created with another member. See how you and your Board score...and what you would prioritise:

- Group and individual respect
- A balance of skills, respected by each other
- An understanding of the business (or an essential part of the business)
- A willingness to get involved, not interfere, but to be used by the management
- No ego
- Willing to assess risk and not to be risk averse
- A desire to get to know the whole team (staff, volunteers, creatives)

- To like each other, or at least be comfortable to be open with each other
- You accept that each person speaks a different language – the language of finance, law, theatre, education, funding agency – and wish to develop a suitable babel fish/translation together so we each understand more of the other's lingo
- Time
- A wish to see the work, and be seen to see the work
- Be an advocate, and ideally having a good address book so you can share your enthusiasm with particularly useful people.

And then came some incredibly powerful key words from around the board retreat table: **selflessness, humility, passion** (for the work, or at the least real respect for the people who passionately create the work), **respect, hearing** (not just listening to other's views), **bravery and a wonderful phrase, "animate not dominate"**.

I went from this very formal structured environment to the fledgling company meeting, where along with a highly respected theatre director also invited to join, I needed to see whether I felt I could be useful. I was deeply impressed. The meeting was informal but structured. It was animated. There was a collective passion and enormous respect expressed for the work and the founding creatives of that work. There was no chair, or need for a chair because everyone was respectful and hearing – an almost natural thinking environment. I could see a skills gap I could help to fill (even if I will almost double the average age of the board!). I could sense passion, and could see already that other highly regarded theatre practitioners and funding bodies had spotted (and supported) this fledgling company.

So why join a Board? For me, it's three things:

- I believe in and respect the passion and skill of the key people involved

- I feel that they (or we) can create **necessary theatre**, which can change lives

- I understand what I can do personally to help.

I'm in, I've signed my Companies House form, and now I'd better start reading some budgets, plays, vision documents, and background to see how I can actually help Metta Theatre. Thanks for inviting me, and thanks for the tea and fantastic brie at lunchtime.

[Three years on, I am slowly coming off the Metta Theatre Board. I am no longer employed by a Board myself because I'm freelance. I am newly on the Board of the Production Exchange and I've just been asked to be on the Board of a new theatre. I feel I have given what I can to Metta, who continue to thrive, and now need to give myself some space.]

Sans Teeth – Second Childishness

I'm not going to dwell on death, but rather look at glorious second childhoods. I don't expect to be able to retire. I expect to be drinking decaf coffee and offering chamomile tea to the next generation of creative artists till the end...or at least that's what I hope.

I have just been to the funeral of Freda Barratt, a Bury St Edmunds actress who, at 87 had just finished doing a walk on cameo in a soap, and an advert for mobile phones playing, as she put it, another "Dotty Old Lady."

Picture the scene. Two old dears getting to grips with their mobile phones over tea. Freda offers the immortal line – "the trouble with predictive text is that you cannot swear." Cut to smiling salesman with the logo of a famous phone shop. Cut back to Freda saying: "See…F..U…" cut.

Freda worked as part of the Authentic Artist Collective on a project called Tender Age, exploring the way in which young adults (16-25) and older people (from 65 +) could meet in creative conversation. There is a wonderful clip of Freda dancing around the rehearsal room with her handbag. Energised. Playing. At one with the music. Glorious.

So instead of dwelling on death, let's go back to the beginning and (with Kath's permission) add a rather useful A-Z of getting into Drama School which she prepared some years ago for "Aim Higher."

As you read this, think now, in second childhood, what else you might suggest to the 18 year old you. Add your thoughts, use this list (with due credit please), make your own and pass us a copy. How can we help and inspire the creative artists of the future?

It would be a pleasure to add other lists covering technical, film, design, opera, ballet or visual art career A-Z's. Please feed through open source lists to add to our websites. Thank you.

FROM KATH BURLINSON/2008

Aim higher A-Z

The A to Z of Auditioning for Drama Schools or University Drama Courses

A: Auditions

Most drama schools will ask you to do one classical speech (pre-1800) and one modern speech (post 1950 or 1960). Musical Theatre (MT) courses will expect two songs plus a classical and modern monologue. You will also be taught a dance routine in MT auditions. It is a very good idea to prepare at least two classical and two modern speeches that show different aspects of what you can do. You may be asked to do more than two and you will look unprofessional if you are not prepared. Same with songs – have four ready that show off what your voice can do, range, style, etc. Universities vary – some may want you to prepare speeches, others ask you to attend a workshop, some just want an interview. Be sure to check in advance!

"Basically you need to be aware that no two auditions will be the same, you may hate one you may love the next, so don't be put off if one goes particularly badly or you got over scared etc. – schools may be looking for slightly different things." (James, Guildford School of Acting)

B: Bard

Most classical speeches performed at auditions are from Shakespeare. Some drama schools will ask you to pick a speech from a pre-given list. If they do, don't use this speech at other schools—you will seem lazy. You can start researching classical speeches by looking at collections of

Shakespeare monologues, **BUT**:

- Be sure to find a speech that suits your age
- Be sure to READ THE WHOLE PLAY and really understand how your speech fits into the plot, why your character is saying what they are saying, and to whom.

You can also look beyond Shakespeare at other Elizabethan and Jacobean playwrights: try Ben Jonson, Webster, Middleton and Dekker, etc. Research and READ!

C: Character

"Character – the closer to your casting the better (eg same age, same accent, same attitude) as what they are really interested in is getting to know the student in the short space they have." (Fiona, Mountview)

One of the biggest mistakes made is not knowing the character or the material well enough. *"When working on your speeches, think about what your character says about themselves, what they say about others, what others say about them. Be specific!"* (Tutor, LAMDA)

The more you know about the character, the more choices you have. Think about the 5 W's—Who What When Where Why? What does your character want? What is s/he trying to communicate? How does s/he try to get what s/he wants? Whose behaviour is s/he trying to change?

D: Drama Schools

There are 22 drama schools that are part of the Conference of Drama Schools: www.drama.ac.uk

These schools are considered by many in the profession to be the "top" schools. But some have recently merged with universities, expanded enormously, increased the numbers of students they accept and reduced the contact hours, so do your research! You can download a lot of information from the website about the various courses.

Do not rule out schools that are not CDS...they may be more suited to you.

E: Ever Such Hard Work!

In our star-based culture, drama schools are not on the lookout for the wannabes, the arrogant, the people who think they are pretty/handsome/fabulous—drama schools do NOT want these people.

"I think it's important people know the reality of how tough the training actually is – numerous people in my year suffered depression and eating disorders due to stess etc." (Sophie, Guildford School of Acting) With this message in mind check the support and counselling systems that are in place. Some schools make a key feature of ensuring they offer support to the whole person, and not just their immediate performing skills. Others may not be so specific.

"I think it's important for students to decide if they really want to pursue a career in theatre or not...because drama school can push people out of their comfort zones in a lot of ways and those that are not focussed on what they want tend to view these pushes as negative ones. So to sum up I'd say that if you do want to come to drama school then you need to be 100% focussed on it." (Jaygann, Guildford School of Acting)

"Drama school is HARD work! Long hours, early mornings, lots of extra work, lots of extra reading and the tutors expect 100% commitment all the time. And it is STRICT! Three people have already been thrown off my course for lateness and absenteeism. Two other people have had written warnings about their professional demeanour and attitude. It is not a walk in the park!" (Fiona, Mountview)

F: Friendliness

When you are at auditions, try to make friends with other people. You may be able to find out very useful information about other places they have auditioned. There may also be students around who are already studying at the drama school/uni—ask them what it's like! Ask them what you want to know—how many hours singing per week? Is there much dance? What is the voice work like? Who are the best teachers there? Which courses are good?

On the other hand:

"A fundamental thing that would have been good to know before my auditions, is not to be put off by what other people say, for example if someone at an audition says 'they only expect blonde dancers at this school' etc don't listen and never change what you have practised, don't let anyone influence what you have rehearsed." (James, Guildford School of Acting)

G: Games and Improvisation

At some drama schools and university group auditions, you may be asked to play some theatre games. Enjoy yourself, listen carefully to the instructions and concentrate. Be generous and responsive to others.

"The games are special drama games which test things such as focus and concentration – don't take them too seriously, just have fun with them and be creative in whatever you are doing." (James, Mountview)

In some drama school recalls and at university auditions you may be asked to improvise. Do not try to be funny. Try to be open, responsive, to listen to your partner/s, to accept offers. At some schools, you may be asked to create a duologue with someone else, using your monologues— so creating a scene that is made up of two different and unrelated scripts. This will test how you think on your feet, how you listen, whether you can be creative.

"At my auditions a lot of schools asked you to do impro in groups and the best thing I can say is accept everything that's presented in impro—don't block an idea—only makes things harder for yourself and people notice." Natasha (Colchester Institute – Performing Arts)

H: Happiness

You may be very nervous, but it's important to smile, to look as though you are enjoying yourself. After all, this is supposed to be what you love to do!

"Smile and be yourself. I remember when I started my head of dance said she remembered me from my audition because I was relaxed and smiled, she was able to gauge from that the type of person I was and the attitude I had, so yeah...smile!" (James, Mountview)

I: Interviews

At drama schools and universities, you are likely to be interviewed.

"The most improvisatory part of the auditions for me tended to be the interviews, where I found myself answering questions that I could not have possibly prepared for. I would have liked to have more practice at interview technique as I personally struggled with these. This includes having solid answers and views on aspects of the theatre and what I see happening in my career – difficult questions I'm sure you'll agree!" (Fiona, Mountview)

"In interview I want to know why I should take them – and then what they could offer the college. I want to be confident that they're confident not arrogant – I'm on the look out for the ones who are 'stars' in their own family. I want to see

how they take constructive criticism." (Tutor, Musical Theatre Academy)

"Interview technique – don't try to be anyone other than yourself, listen to the question and answer it without rambling. If you can't answer it, say so. Have some sensible questions ready about the programme. Try to relax and be yourself." (Tutor, University of Hull)

J: Jitters

You will be nervous on the day. Make sure to connect with your breath, to be as centred as you can. Warm up your voice, massage your face, move your tongue around your mouth before you go in. And breathe. Keep breathing. Our breath is the first thing to go wrong when we are nervous, and is the key to finding calm again. Breathe.

K: Sarah Kane

A lot of people choose a Sarah Kane monologue for their modern speech. Don't. They are over-used. A lot of schools suggest you also avoid Berkoff. Also, tutors get fed up with listening to speech after speech that is gloomy and depressed or overly violent.

(Tutor: LAMDA) "I would say avoid: Dead babies, Rape, Mental illness, Doom and gloom"

You may think these sorts of speeches are "dramatic", but imagine having to listen to one after another, all day long!

L: Learning

"Know your pieces so so so well, this let me down!" (Olenka, Northumbria University). You need to know your speeches/ songs inside out and so well that nothing will throw you, even if you are asked to perform it in an entirely different way (which you might). You may well be questioned by tutors on any aspect of your speeches or songs.

"It was kind of like a bad cop good cop routine. They asked you questions about why you chose the speeches, why acting, why this course, etc. Some people who weren't prepared were kind of left exposed." (Linda, Central School of Speech and Drama)

M: Monologues

Read details about audition pieces very carefully, especially length of piece, number of pieces, type of pieces.

Good bookshops to find monologues: Samuel French produce *The Guide to Selecting Plays for Performance*, French's Theatre Bookshop, 52 Fitzroy Street, London W1P 6JR, Tel. 0207 387 9373.

Also The National Theatre Bookshop, Upper Ground, South Bank London SE1 9PX Tel. 0207 928 2033

Choose a piece that shows who you are and what you can do. Don't try to be something that you think they want. Use your own accent.

"Be yourself and don't try and be someone else for anyone." (Bex, RSAMD).

"Choose something close to yourself, something believable, but also try and look for monologues that not everyone will be doing." (Linda, Central)

"Before you begin you will be asked your name, where you are from, the acting piece you are doing and where it is from, the name of the character and the name of the author – speak clearly – don't get up and be shy and mumble – it won't give a good impression." (James, Mountview)

(Tutor, Central) My advice is:

"Don't make life difficult for yourself! Choose a piece that is near you in age, gender. Avoid accents that are hard to do, e.g Liverpool, Geordie! Avoid anything strongly identified with a particular actress, e.g Julie Walters! Don't try to shock, e.g. Equus!

Think about you. What kind of person are you? What are your strengths, what kind of piece will make you feel confident, that you'll enjoy.

Find contrasting pieces, e.g. I can be energised and funny AND still and thoughful! If you can be!

It is useful for one piece to have a character talking to another."

N: Never Never

Get your monologues by downloading them from the internet. There may be no play to go with it! If asked questions about the piece, you will look very silly, and very lazy.

O: Open Days

Go to them! Look around! Get the feel of the place. Ask questions. Find out as much as you can. Does this feel like a place you would like to be for three years of your life?

P: Preparation Preparation Preparation

Preparation is CRUCIAL. If you have not prepared properly, it will show.

"...What I think is most important is to be prepared because it's fairly competitive and you can instantly spot the people who aren't prepared. I think they are looking for a level of maturity and artistic integrity as well as talent." (Linda, Central)

Follow the advice above about learning your speeches/ songs inside out. Know your character and their part in the play. Practise your monologues/songs in many different ways: laughing all the way through, as if drunk, very depressed, very panicky, etc. It will stretch you, keep the pieces alive and you may find out something interesting.

Know as much as you can about the college/course. Do your research. Make sure you understand the terms being used. For example, Music Theatre and Musical Theatre are not the same thing!

"Common mistakes include not knowing the pieces well enough, not knowing anything about them, not knowing the college enough (so they can't adjust their answers to fit the surroundings)." Tutor (Musical Theatre Academy)

Q: Questions

Ask them! Some schools provide FAQs Frequently Asked Questions...but you may have other questions to ask staff or current students. *"Make a list of your top five things to ask. Speak to admin staff. Ask the same question to 3 or 4 people. If the school says it runs masterclasses, ask what that means. Is that industry professionals coming in? Who?"* (Lee, London School of Musical Theatre)

R: Recalls

If you get a recall, well done! Schools may have one or more recalls (RADA has an initial audition and three recalls before final acceptance). You may be asked to participate in a workshop, do the same or different speeches, sing a song, move or dance or do some physical theatre, do duologues with existing students, anything!

"The second round was later in the day and the panel then consisted of the rest of the people on the panel and also two students that were there to work with you. In this round you had to do your second Shakespeare, they also worked on your other Shakespeare. To me it felt like this one was to see if you were flexible and open to direction also how you worked with other people aka the students. They kept giving me different ideas of how to play with the monologues and how to think about the character." (Linda, Central)

"First Audition quick chat, speeches, further chat

Second Audition meet more important people, speeches, song, chat

3rd Shakespeare workshop, Chekhov workshop, some improvisation (just about being open and responsive, not being funny)

4th new speech, dance, impro perform to everybody." (Michael, RADA)

(Tutor: Central) *"Remember that drama schools are not looking for a trained actor, but someone who will benefit from their training, i.e. people with energy, enthusiasm, concentration, a sense of play, of fun, mentally flexible, able to listen, take direction, be thoughtful, cooperative, caring, with a real interest in theatre and, very importantly, who can create the world of the character and share the story."*

S: Songs

If you are auditioning for Musical Theatre, songs are obviously hugely important.

"Make sure both songs are completely contrasting and take a 3rd just in case they don't like your choices. If I was doing the audition again I would research everything about the songs I was doing, the character, the musical, who it is by, based on anything? what theatre it was on at? why I chose it, other musicals the writers have written. I would do one belting one and one head voice. In the auditions they want to see what you are like most of all so make one of your songs quite close to you. and the other a character song. It is advised not to sing Sondheim or Jason Robert Brown songs as their piano accompaniment is really difficult and you wouldn't be able to guarantee that the pianist could play it perfectly straight off. Try to find rare material, so that other people in the audition don't have the same songs as you, this means you won't be compared, also shows that you

have researched more. Also songs that are associated with other people are a bad choice eg. Memory – Elaine Paige or anything from Evita." (Becky, Trinity College of Music)

"My advice with the singing audition would be to make sure that you know everything about your character that you could possibly find out, obviously have a good understanding of the show and most importantly just get up and be confident, at the end of the day the panel are just normal people as well and they really only want you to do well! Some people don't like you staring at them or delivering the entire song to them so it might be an idea to ask if you sing the song to them or out to the audience." (James, Mountview)

"At my GSA audition they quizzed us all on Musical Theatre asking us to name a musical and then asking us if it was fact or fictional. And so many people didn't have a clue." Natasha (Colchester Institute)

"I look for people that have a modicum of talent but more importantly really 'want it'. By that I mean that they are really passionate about Musical Theatre – so I need to know that they've seen lots of it (even if it's just on film), have a Musical Theatre idol – that sort of thing. I'm looking out for the wannabes (obviously to avoid them like the plague). For their audition material I want to know why they chose it. Song choices – they tend to do pieces not suitable for their age/experience.

My standard questions incl: what show if any would you be in? What part in that show? Where do they see their strengths/weaknesses?" (Tutor, Musical Theatre Academy)

T: Taking Direction

If a school is interested in you, they will want to see if you can take direction. So be prepared to do your speeches in different ways, accept suggestions, try things out, LISTEN to what is being asked of you. You may have to think on your feet.

"Some of my friends who were auditioning were asked to change certain parts of their speech and perform them again in different ways so this can happen and it is important to be prepared to be flexible with your choices. Having speeches 'worked' by the panel usually occurrs in second and third rounds of auditions." (Fiona, Mountview)

"In Musical Theatre recalls, expect them to ask you to sing a song in a different way, they might play around with it and give you something to do with the song. For example they might put you in a scenario and get you to sing it in these circumstances. This is really to see how well you can or cannot take direction and perform." (James, Mountview)

U: University Drama

There are many university drama courses available— which are all different from one another, so once again, do your research! Older universities tend to ask for higher grades than new universities. Most courses will be based on a mixture of practical and academic study, but the emphasis will vary, so check it out!

"I enjoyed the uni's which gave you a more personal introduction to the course. Most were similiar, involving games then exercises, often requiring an element of physical theatre and group work. I very nearly applied to drama school instead but based on my experiences I'd say if you have the ability to get into a top university and study drama, do it. As it is so much fun and you meet so many people who don't just want to be on the stage! I'm very happy on my drama course at Exeter which I would highly recommend to anyone who wants to study Drama at degree level and wants a great balance of practical and theory based work." (James, University of Exeter)

"The biggest difference between the universities and drama schools was the universities wanted you to see how their department worked but the drama schools were purely auditioning you...Finding out how many hours you're in is important. At the audition they explained all the modules and they sounded really interesting but then they were just over exaggerated!" (Olenka, Northumbria University)

"If you are unsure what area of theatre to go into, University is great as you are allowed to experiment in first year with every area of acting and backstage work, and then you can shadow a professional in Second year and in 3rd year you are able to work in your specialised area, funded by the university... (well thats how Queens works)" (Lynne, Queen's University Belfast)

"I think the course at Bath Spa is a very good course. It has a lot of variety as we do acting, comedy (fooling/clowning and Dario Fo for first year, commedia and stand up for second year), physical theatre, movement, stage combat, voice and body and choral lessons– these are all active up on your feet lessons, so it's not a course I'd recommend to anyone who is not ready to really go through it physically and mentally.

As well as the course being very practical we are encouraged to be 'thinking' actors so there is a fair amount of written work to back up the practical so we can interrogate our process and practice. To enable us to have stage management skills, design skills etc etc we do 2 hours theatre craft a week. There are also contextual lessons where we look deeper into the text we are working on in our acting classes (2 hours a week).

At the moment the course works out as 25 hours contact time a week so it is very busy – including self directed rehearsals for acting it works out as 9-6 everyday, and then with extra productions it works out as a very long day! Most of my days are 9-9!! But I love it." (Grace, Bath Spa)

"Universities can't afford to be as picky as they used to be – lots more courses and no more students. But we look for a willingness to take part/contribute, without being over-pushy, flexibility – being prepared to try things in a practical class and follow a new line of argument in seminar, sensitivity to the group in both seminar and practical. In a word 'teachability'. Nothing puts people off more than someone who thinks they already know more than us." (Tutor, University of Hull)

"The hardest part to do was, far and away, the personal statement. It's really important to make it personal and not just another essay that they've seen before." (Hannah, currently applying to universities)

V: Very Difficult Industry!

"If there was one thing I wish I'd known in advance it would be: how many graduates of the potential drama school I'd be auditioning for get agents or more importantly work! I feel that this is important as this usually tells you how the industry view graduates from that particular drama school." Jaygann (Guildford School of Acting)

"I think it's helpful to check the schools standing in the industry as well as looking for the right course for you. You just get better exposure at the more prestigous drama schools, they sell you better. Saying that I have friends who went to places like E15 etc and they are doing really well and then there are people at my course who are no longer acting so you never can tell. Also check the teaching staff, as that is kind of what you are paying for. I found it to be inspiring to have teachers who would go off and voice coach Nick Cage or Meryl Streep or do movement for Luc Besson or whatever. It meant they were in demand in the industry plus were up to date with what was going on as well." (Linda, Central)

"It can never be over emphasised just how hard it is going

to be – our head of acting said just the other day, out of the 40 in my year only two or three will go on to work regularly enough to make a living from acting!" (Fiona, Mountview)

W: Websites

All drama schools and colleges have websites. This is the obvious place to start your research. Also look at:

www.drama.ac.uk the website for the Conference of Drama Schools

www.thestage.co.uk is the website for the industry paper, also has a discussion forum

www.getintotheatre.org is a national website with lots of info on all aspects of theatre.

X: Xyster

Is there a word or phrase in your monologue that you don't fully understand? Then FIND OUT! Use good editions for your Shakespeare, eg, the Arden editions, which have good notes to help you with unfamiliar words and concepts. Don't try and "wing it" – it won't work!

Y: *Your* school or uni?

"I think it is helpful to form an opinion about the college beforehand, attend an open day or speak to someone there. I think it's important to find the one that's right for you. I knew instantly after the auditions that Central was the place for me and I think that that is an important feeling when you start the course." (Linda, Central)

"I think it is so very very important for each artist to do as much research as possible on the schools – visiting them, attending open days, talking to current students, reading prospectuses in order to determine whether this course is the right one for them." Fiona (Mountview)

"Read the information about the Schools carefully. Choose schools that you think offer the right length course and that appeal to you. If you can, go and see some of the student performances. You can phone the school for details of programe." (Tutor, Central)

Z: Zebra striped bodysuits

You may be asked to move at auditions – so wear loose, comfortable clothing. Some schools make specific suggestions about what to wear. Avoid constricting clothing! It is better to go for a more neutral look than a "hello look at me" style that will get in the way of your work.

If you are auditioning for Musical Theatre courses, you will be expected to dance.

"For the dance audition you will be asked to wear dance wear or something that you can move in if you are not a dancer. The group took part in a short dance style warm-up (stretching etc.) and then were split in two groups. One group consisted of people who considered themselves strong dancers and one who weren't. We then learned a routine in our groups. The routines are usually only a minute or so long. Obviously if you are a strong dancer you will probably know what to expect, for the non– dancers the routine is much more simple and it's only there to see how you can move and how you perform – again, they only want you to do well. One thing that they look out for is performance and style. If you mess up your dance but still deliver it with a sense of the style and maybe even a character they will be really impressed. Even if it goes totally wrong, make it up as long as it's in the style of the music! They will love it! If you aren't a dancer it is a really good idea to take lessons in jazz, tap, and ballet before your audition, this will help you a lot with the audition however it is not essential." (James, Mountview)

Going to drama school or university will cost a lot of money.

Even the auditions and travel will cost a lot.

Be prepared—you might be better off working for a while, gaining experience before auditioning. Some drama schools prefer people with some life experience behind them.

"First time you apply go for the 3 you really want to get into– £30-£40 an audition – plus travel – costs a lot – I auditioned for 8 first time round – not one recall. If you don't get in first time take a gap year or two – get life experience, work as a cleaner, as a clown, behind a bar – anything, start living – schools are interested in interesting people." (Grace, Bath Spa)

and finally...

Never Let Anyone Tread On Your Dreams

GOOD LUCK!

Thanks to Kath and all the artists who shared their current drama school experience with her back in 2008. Of the names I spot and know – one has completed 2 seasons at the RSC and 4 shows at the National Theatre, two are teaching, another is working in PR. One is currently covering Javert in *Les Misérables*, another is understudying Carlotta in *Phantom of the Opera*, a third has been a principal in *Avenue Q* in the West End. One is working as a burlesque artist, another has been in a number of shows for the Norwegian National Theatre company and a third is working on cruises. You just never know.

A few agitations from an old codger – with a few teeth

At the sixth or seventh age of man, I guess we are allowed to challenge the current way things are working, and ask questions which maybe no-one will answer. All I hope is that they are offered as agitations which are meant for the common good:

a) Government and the Arts

b) Ticket Pricing

c) The West End is not the only place for the arts

d) Respecting Musical Theatre

BLOG 130615

Am I getting arts funding all wrong...?

What do I teach the next generation of cultural leaders about politicians and government attitudes to arts? It's a genuine question and I am at a loss of how to tackle it. UK students arrive at class enthused by the possibility of the creative arts, with a sense that everything is possible. The international cohort arrives, believing the arts represent the pinnacle of achievement in the UK of which everyone must be rightly proud. They want to learn best practice and return to excite their own creative worlds in Taiwan, China, Russia, Italy, France, Kenya, Germany, Brazil and beyond.

But what do I teach them? Why don't politicians and UK government advisors seem to get it? How do I explain the principal of creative and economic starvation?

I think I must be a bear of little brain.

Here in the UK, we have a vibrant industry with massive employment. It in turn generates massive further employment in the service sector, tourism, and the product supply side (beer and ice cream, to name but two).

Each year, some r&d money is pumped into the creative businesses across the UK to enable them to develop new product, and some monies are pumped in to enable the business to sell its product more widely (more inclusively) and serve a less accessible public. The purchases made by these customers cause a flow of VAT back to the revenue which, as I understand it, exceeds the level of the r&d investment made by local authorities and the government agencies.

So we have major employers, resulting in profitable return on investment to the government – and a business which can grow, expand, export, and generate even more return and employment given a bit of seed corn.

Employment and profit surely speak to our current government, so why not do more, and make more, rather than do less and make less?

There is more good news for the government…

The businesses which have r&d support also train people who will go on to work in the commercial sector where no r&d is needed. Then the products they create commercially will feed monies back to the revenue "now and forever", to misquote Cats? So r&d this year and next will generate multiple returns for 10-20 years, plus potential exports.

And there's more good news for the government…

Theatre is a business that helps the health and wellbeing of the people of this nation. It brings joy. It tackles challenging issues. It offers cathartic collective experiences. It takes young people off the streets to create meaningful creativity. It takes beauty and joy into hospitals. Many studies have shown that if people experience joy and can explore their problems, then they don't get sick so much, and so they don't need doctors or hospitals so much, and they don't take time off work so much – so the government saves more money and makes more tax revenues.

And there's more good news for the government….

This business works with young people in schools. It brings history, English literature, science, geography, art, and our culture to life. It makes it easier for young people to pass exams.

It gives them confidence to speak out and go for interviews. It gives them a skill in teamwork and helps to make leaders. So for the government, this tiny r&d is spreading out potential revenue earning for the government for a whole generation and beyond.

Maybe I'd better stop there...I haven't even talked about the inherent need for, and joy in, exploring our own cultural and creative potential – or even suggested "art for arts' sake."

Now – how do I explain all this to my cohort of highly intelligent international future cultural leaders? How do I explain death by a thousand cuts? How do I explain that the government just doesn't like the arts, and that governments and local authorities can't think about the future of this country and its citizens when they have to focus on the next election? Is that the answer? Is that what I should be teaching? What a shame if it is.

I'd welcome your help on this one – especially if you are an MP, civil servant, local councillor or think-tanker. Do let me know. Thanks so much.

Chris / Course Leader – MA Arts Management / Anglia Ruskin University.

[Since writing this Blog Anglia Ruskin has sadly stopped its MA Arts Management course, because more international students are needed to attend and make the course pay better. No worries. The questions above still apply, and my request for wise understanding still holds true. In the future, I will be running the MA in Creative Producing at Mountview and would love to offer a much clearer, less pessimistic, view of the future to my cohorts of UK and International cultural leaders.]

BLOG 120319

Theatre as a luxury item, or bargain hunter's challenge

Kevin Spacey has set some discussions running about the price of West End tickets. Almost all the copy I've seen has been focused on London, and there has been good coverage of major London sponsorship schemes to make theatre accessible to Under 26s and other groups. All good. Speaking personally, [ie without the benefit of marketing study or a look at the phenomenal statistics that Michael Quine and the TMA (now UK Theatre) produce on theatre income trends] I sense that theatre prices outside the West End have not changed that much. My memory of 20 years ago, running Buxton Opera House, is that we might charge £16-£18 for a touring drama, and now at the Theatre Royal Bury St Edmunds we charge £20 best seats. And we, like so many theatres outside London's West End, are absolutely determined to encourage U26 and new audiences to try a visit to the theatre. We offer an advance purchase ticket for a play at £8.50, so young people might take a chance, just as they might with a trip out to the cinema. For me, theatre should not be an exclusive "special occasion" in the way we promote it – because an occasion feels like something an average person might feel excluded from. I want someone to come and see a play because it's a night out, some fun, an experience [or a piece of Necessary Theatre]...not something they need to dress up for, or combine with a candle-lit dinner for two. So thank you Mr Spacey for gaining valuable column inches, as only a celebrity can, for this discussion to be aired...and let's expand the discussion to non-West End prices. And also let's celebrate the accessible pricing on the London Fringe.

My blog title had two parts. I'm also saddened by the "bargain hunter" mentality in the West End now. I guess the two go hand in hand. Set the ticket prices high, and then dump a load through Last Minute schemes or to club schemes. Just like hotels, there seems to be the rack rate, and the rate a person in the know can get a ticket for. However the simple fact of having the "in the know" rate again makes the act of getting a theatre ticket an exclusive act [and I should add I seem to be one of those people who never is "in the know", and all my theatre colleagues tell me how they would never pay full price...you just ask x, or use y club, or join z]. Wouldn't it be wonderful if, like the non West End theatre, prices were set as low as possible to sell to the widest audience at that rate – and not to hike the rates higher and higher just to sell them off at a bargain.

Maybe the marketing-man inside of me should love the complexity of finding the best way to ensure people pay the price they can afford, however high that is. But my sense is that the balance between luxury exclusivity and bargain basement has got out of hand, and is damaging the chance to attract new audiences to see live theatre.

If I'm out of touch, have straw between my ears from too much regional theatre, or I am just plain wrong as a marketing man, then tell me quickly. I am currently working with my colleagues at Bury St Edmunds to try to reduce the top price, and tighten the margins between best/exclusive and cheapest/most affordable. The reason is to make it look less pricey, less exclusive, more accessible.

[PS – written a year after this blog. The pricing restructure did work – we increased attendance and per ticket yield, and the perception was that we were more affordable. Some consultants buzzing around us at the time thought we were mad. We stuck to our guns and it worked.]

BLOG 130206

Is there any new inspiration in theatre ....?

There are so often cries that the West End is filled with star classics, megamixes and old musicals. If that's your impression (it's not mine), then you need to challenge yourself to go outside Zone 2 and seek more diversity. Whilst it is likely that *The Mousetrap* and *Stomp* will continue to be on the doorstep of the Ivy for many years, and your path from the Groucho is likely to take you past *Miss Saigon* for some time to come, there is exciting new stuff happening for you to discover.

Firstly let me put a marker down that the above challenge is not lain at the doors of the main journalistic critics of the theatre. They are already trying to pack 6-8 shows a week into their lives, and time to write and observe the political scene as it unfolds across the nation and beyond. My challenge is to all of us who go to the theatre and then tweet, blog, chat about what we've seen. It's easy for everyone to explore the merits or otherwise of *Viva Forever* or *The Bodyguard*, I put in a plea for all of us to look over the edge...

Last night I was at a powerful, disturbing and stonkingly well acted new play by Tim Luscombe. This was a far cry from his beautiful adaptation of *Mansfield Park* produced by the Theatre Royal Bury St Edmunds. Last night was *Kimalia*, commissioned by Mountview Academy of Theatre, and premiered with fine direction by Anthony Lau and a beautiful stage setting by Rhys McDowell. Drama schools can, and do, take risks by bringing to the stage new and challenging work. They have the luxury of big cohorts of diverse actors, and last night was a treat. I will give nothing away except to say that you will be disturbed by much of the (true) content on asylum seekers, and you will be challenged with your expectations on gender and sexual relations. On a day when same sex marriage was passing through a stormy be-suited House of Commons, the Mountview students were looking at the underbelly of a love which, in many countries, dare not speak its name – let alone walk down the aisle. *Kimalia* runs till Saturday at the Bernie Grant Centre, 3 minutes walk from Seven Sisters Station, which is 15 minutes on the Victoria Line from Oxford Circus. Have an adventure...and if you're early I recommend the Spanish Omelette and a mug of tea at Charley's Café.

But there's more... On Monday I had a free night. I tweeted to see who of my followers had ideas for me. Top tips came back, including Vertical Line Theatre's *Lineup* at Greenwich Theatre. I hadn't been to Greenwich for ages, and it seemed a perfectly crazy thing to do – go see a new company doing 7 scratch new plays – they probably need some cheering along on a dark Monday night in the big house of Greenwich Theatre.

I arrived. The bar was packed. The audience was buzzing. And by the time we sat down I was bemused to see a completely full house. We watched 7 extraordinarily tight pieces of new writing by Olga Nikora, Caroline Dixev, Lucinda Burnett, Jonathan Skinner, Stacey Haber and David Hofberg, Elizabeth Muncey, and Andrew Maddock. I don't remember ever seeing a scratch night without a dud...surely that's to be expected. There wasn't one dud. I know little about the writers. I learned a little about Vertical Line from the ever-resourceful James Haddrell, director of Greenwich Theatre and champion of this and many young companies. Created by Henry Regan, Ross Stanley and joined by Producer Steph Connell they grew out of directing programmes in London, and featured recent drama school graduates given some cracking material to get their teeth into. The event is a great opportunity for casting directors and emerging producers to see 22 actors who have been auditioned and gathered for their skill with new work. And my sense is that almost all are eminently cast-able. James gave the new company the theatre for the day. The company did an amazing job packing the theatre. And the audience in turn fed back some funds into the theatre's coffers by drinking a goodly amount of beer, wine and brandy. I will most definitely try and find their next date in 2 months time, and be back. They are planning to be in Edinburgh this year so check out their website www.verticallinetheatre.co.uk

I am delighted that Greenwich council has seen the value of the arts in their area and confirmed with James that they will not be culling their arts spend. The young people and residents of Greenwich are in a better place than those in Somerset, Newcastle, Westminster and others who are slashing support for the Arts. I wish Social Services and all those who support the people of Somerset, Newcastle and Westminster well with their citizens in the long-term. Savings on the arts today will have a long-term effect. It will take 5-10 years for the real effects of arts cuts to be felt by communities, by which time I am sure all our noble politicians will be in the Lords or back on the Boards of international industry. Those who then run Greenwich Theatre, or Bernie Grant Centre, or Vertical Line Theatre will continue to be struggling to support the communities they serve. And writers from Tim Luscombe to those seen at the scratch will continue, I hope, to challenge us to think about our world, on the edge, beyond Zone 2.

Conclusion – Despairing / Stuck

The sixth age shifts
Into the lean and **slippered pantaloon**,
With spectacles on nose and pouch on side,
His youthful hose, well saved, a world too wide
For his shrunk shank, and his big, manly voice,
Turning again toward childish treble, pipes
And whistles in his sound. Last scene of all,
That ends this strange, eventful history,
Is **second childishness** and mere oblivion,
Sans teeth, sans eyes, sans taste, sans everything.

Here are 10 thoughts which flow from the last two sections:

Despairing / Stuck

1. Explore Open Space in your work/life

2. Look to nature and the world for new inspiration

3. Consider a creative workshop to stretch your practice

4. Listen to yourself

5. Listen to others

6. Could you support a Board or network?

7. Share the A-Z of drama schools

8. Question what is happening to our world

9. Think about a CGO Surgery/or giving feedback

10. Thank you for reading.

Epilogue – Thank you

As is my wont, I have gone on longer than I expected. I have used more of the Blogs to illustrate and explore different ideas. My thanks to the Arts Council in London for encouraging me to put in a small bid to support the CGO Surgeries, and to include a way to bring some of my experience of my life in theatre to a wider audience. I didn't expect to be publishing a book. I am delighted to be doing so, and I hope those who look and review my Grant for the Arts feedback will be happy with this development.

In the next few months I will be gaining more skills and eventually a Diploma in Personal Coaching. I am already offering my pre-diploma services with some inspiring people across the UK. My intention is to use the skills I have gained over 30 years in the theatre business, across a much wider portfolio of businesses.

This book has touched on my interest in wellness and holistic approaches to healing and life. I believe that the arts can play a central place in the improvement of the lives of people on this planet. I hope we are in time to make a difference. I look forward to helping those who are at the forefront of new developments which improve lives, enrich life and empower people across all communities.

Thank you for exploring this array of blogs and thoughts
I hope you will find it useful
Do get in contact
All good wishes
Chris
chris@chrisgrdy.org

Bibliography

"How to" books

Botting, N. and Norton, M., (2012) *The Complete Fundraising Handbook*, 6th edition. Directory of Social Change – CG

Fisher, M., (2012) *The Edinburgh Fringe Survival Guide: How to Make Your Show A Success*

Green, J., (2012) *How to Produce A West End Show*, Oberon Books – CG

Hill, E., O'Sullivan, C. and O'Sullivan, T., (2003) *Creative Arts Marketing*, Butterworth Heinemann – CG

Salt, C., (2001) *Make Acting Work – the practical path to a successful career*, (2nd Edition) Methuen

Seabright, J.,(2010) *So You Want To Be A Theatre Producer?*, London, Nick Hern Books – CG

Volz, J., (2010) *How to Run A Theatre*, (2nd Edition) Bloomsbury

Woolford, J., (2012) *How Musicals Work*, Nick Hern Books

Essential Reference Book: (2013) *Contacts*, Spotlight

UK cultural management

I am grateful for this list of works to my colleagues Pam Pffromer, Professor Henry Lydiate, other past teachers on the old MA Arts Management course at Anglia Ruskin, to Kath Burlinson, and to my new colleagues on the MA

Creative Producing for Mountview Academy of Theatre. I have highlighted (CG) the ones that I have read/have on my shelves for regular reference at home:

Bolton, R., and Bolton, D.G., (2009) *People Styles at Work*, Amacom – Kindle CG

Booker, C., (2004) *The Seven Basic Plots*, Continuum – CG

Casey, B., Dunlop, R., and Selwood, S. (1996) *Culture As Commodity*, Policy Studies Institute

Cashman, S., (2003) *Thinking BIG! The conceptual guide to strategy, marketing and planning*, Arts Marketing Association – CG

Chong, D., (2008) *Arts Management*, London, Routledge

Cowling, J., (ed) (2004) *For Art's Sake: society and the arts in the 21st century*, London, Institute for Public Policy Research

Dyson Jr., (2010) *Accounting for Non Accounting Students*, Prentice Hall

Farber, D.C., (2006) *Producing Theatre*, Limelight Editions – CG

Fitzgibbon, M., (2001) *Managing Innovation in the Arts*, Quorum Books

Freeman, J., (2010) *Blood, Sweat & Theory*, Libri Publishing – CG

French, A., Traynor, T., Smyth, J., Chronnell, C., Carver, J., Lillya, D., and Johnston, S., (2010) *The Directory of Grant Making Trusts* 2010/11, 21st Edition Directory of Social Change – CG

Harvie, J., (2009) *Theatre and the City*, Palgrave MacMillan

Hesmondhalgh, D., (2007) *The Cultural industries*, Sage – Kindle CG

Hill, L. and Whitehead, B., (2004) *The Complete Membership Handbook*, Directory of Social Change

Hudson, M., (2009) *Managing Without Profit* DSC – CG

Jacobson, D., (1998) *Survival Jobs*, Broadway Books

Kershaw, B. and Nicholson H., (2013) *Research Methods in Theatre and Performance* Edinburgh University Press – CG

Kotler, P. and Scheff, J., (1997) *Standing Room Only*, Harvard Business School Press – CG

Leavy, P., (2009) *Method Meets Arts*, Guilford Publishing

Lloyd, T., (2013) *Why Rich People Give*, Association of Charitable Foundations – CG

Mileham, P., (1995) *Coming on Board*, Institute of Management

Norton, M. and Eastwood, M., (2010) *Writing Better Fundraising Applications, a practical guide*, 4th ed. Directory of Social Change

O'Reilly, D. and Kerrigan, F., (ed) (2010) *Marketing the Arts – a fresh approach*, Routledge – Kindle

Palmer, P., et al., (2005) *The Good Financial Management Guide For The Voluntary Sector*, NCVO

Rodenburg, P., (2007) *Presence*, Penguin – CG

Salt, C., (2003) *Make Acting Work*, (2nd Edition) Berg 3PL – CG

Smith, C., (1998) *Creative Britain*, Faber and Faber

Vogler, C., (2007) *The Writer's Journey*, Michael Weise Productions – CG

Walmsley, B., (2001) *Key Issues in the Arts and Entertainment Industry*, Goodfellow – CG

Think books

The following are a selection of books on my shelves or Kindle which remind me to widen my thinking and question the world. Also they are great sources for quotes, provocation and inspiration. I have added the sub-title to some books to give an indication of the topic covered, where the power-title may not illuminate completely.

Baréz-Brown, C., (2006), *How to have Kick-Ass Ideas – get curious, get adventurous, get creative*, Harper Element – CG

Barsoux, J-L., (1993), *Funny Business – humour, management and business culture*, Casell – CG

Bonham-Carter, D., (2012) *Self-Esteem – a practical guide*, Icon Books – CG

Cantwell, M., (2013) *Be a Free Range Human – escape the 9 to 5...*, Kogan Page – CG

Collins, J., (2001) *Good To Great – why some companies make the leap...and others don't* – CG

Covey, S.R., (2013) *Seven Habits of Highly Effective People* (25th anniversary edition) – Rosetta Books – Kindle CG

Gelb, M.J. and Buzan, T., (1998) *Lessons from the Art of Juggling – how to achieve your full potential in business, learning, and life*, Aurum Press

Goleman, D., (1996) *Emotional Intelligence – why it can matter more than IQ*, Bloomsbury

Hamilton, D.R., (2011) *The Contagious Power of Thinking – how your thoughts can influence the world*, Hay House

Handy, C., (1995) *The Age of Unreason and The Empty Raincoat* – (The Traveller's Companion) Arrow Books – CG

James, B., (2011) *Do It! or Ditch It – Turn ideas into action and make decisions count*, Virgin Books

Klein, N., (2009) *Shock Doctrine – the rise of disaster capitalism*, Knopf Canada – CG

Kline, N., (2011) *Time to Think*, Cassell Illustrated – CG

Lehrer, J., (2012) *Imagine – how creativity works*, Canongate – CG

McGilchrist, I., (2009) *The Master and His Emissary – the divided brain and the making of the western world*, Yale University Press – Kindle CG

Mearns, D. and Thorne, B., (1999) *Person-Centred Counselling in Action*, 2nd Edition Sage Publications

Pearl, S., (2012) *Instructions for Happiness and Success* – *100% guaranteed*, Quadrille Publishing – CG

Torr, G., (2008) *Managing Creative People – Lessons in leadership for the ideas economy*, John Wiley & Sons – Kindle

Westley, F., Zimmerman, B. and Patton, M.Q., (2007) *Getting to Maybe – how the world is changed*, Vintage Canada – CG

Whitmore, J., (2009) *Coaching for Performance – GROWing human potential and purpose*, (4th edition) Nicholas Brealey Publishing – Kindle CG

Wright, S., Holden, J., Kieffer, J. and Newbigin, J. (ed), (2011) *Creativity Money Love – Learning for the 21st century*, self-published with Creative and Cultural Skills and New Direction – CG

Chris Grady is available for one-to-one coaching and freelance consulting.

For more information please contact Chris at:
www.ChrisGrady.org
chris@chrisgrady.org

Index